Dialogic Style in Preaching

GEORGE W. SWANK

MORE EFFECTIVE PREACHING SERIES

Judson Press® Valley Forge

DIALOGIC STYLE IN PREACHING

Library of Congress Cataloging in Publication Data

Swank, George W.
   Dialogic style in preaching
   Includes bibliographical references.
     1. Preaching. 2. Communication (Theology)
I. Title.
BV4211.2.S9   251   81-11778
ISBN 0-8170-0922-1   AACR2

The name JUDSON PRESS is registered as a trademark in the U.S. Patent Office. Printed in the U.S.A. ⊕

TO RUTH,

who for twenty-five years
has turned me loose
to see what I could become,
but
who has steadfastly refused
to let me be
less than I already am.

Contents

CHAPTER 1

The Elements

Preaching is an act of worship involving the whole church. While it may appear that the one speaking is the only active person present, with the hearers merely sitting by, the fact of the matter is quite different. When the gospel is preached, the entire congregation is engaged in the making of sermons. One person speaks aloud stimulating the others to reflect inwardly. During the course of reflection, and under the Spirit of Christ, each individual person brings thoughts, hopes, fears, memories, and insights to bear on the specifics of his or her own life. The result is a message which is self-tailored by each one who participates. The ultimate individual messages will be intimate and private, but much more effective than any that the preacher could possibly devise. These messages represent the Christian insights of the people who have prepared them for themselves.

At least that is what *ought* to happen when the gospel is preached. Sometimes it does not. Sometimes the people merely go to sleep. Or they allow their minds to wander aimlessly, returning occasionally to wonder when the final hymn will be announced so they can be on their way.

But it *can* happen. The people can be included in the preaching, so that they are full and active partners in the process though they speak not a word at this time. How this can be accomplished is the subject of this book. But before we consider how to preach inclusively, it is important to think first about why we should do it.

The Hearing

Preaching does not exist without hearers. One may enter an empty sanctuary to practice a sermon, but such an exercise would hardly be considered preaching. Pulpit proclamation is a distinctly social art. How shall the Word be proclaimed unless there is a hearer? The one who hears is as essential as the one who speaks.

A simple illustration reminds us that people today are immersed in scientific technology that affects the way they perceive their world. In 1851 the initial issue of *The New York Times* represented an amazing scoop. It contained news that had been rushed from Europe to Boston by steamer and then to New York by train. People in New York could actually read of European events that were little more than two weeks old! By contrast, President Kennedy was shot at 12:30 P.M. By one o'clock, 68 percent of the adults in the United States—over 75 million people—knew of it. Moreover, 99.8 percent of the nation knew about it by the end of the afternoon.[1] The remotest corners of the world routinely enter our living rooms to be observed while we eat our frozen dinners. Of course there is no guarantee that we will understand what we see, but at least the world is instantly present in the humblest homes; no longer are other parts of our own nation, or even other nations, remote and mysterious.

However, there is an even deeper implication resulting from our scientific age. It is not just that we are immersed in a world of scientific invention. The truth cuts more sharply than that. We have been trained to think as persons of science.

Modern educational practices have now produced two generations of listeners who have been taught that it is not just the answer, but knowing how the answer was reached that is important. Today's congregations are not interested merely in the attractiveness of the preacher's conclusions. They want to be let in on the process by which the conclusions were reached. If that opportunity is denied them, then they are quite likely to withhold any commitment to the conclusions.

More troublesome still is the news that television has actually altered the way we learn. Marshall McLuhan perhaps has articulated the fundamental changes brought about by electronics better than anyone else. At least he is the most widely quoted!

McLuhan observes that print media cause us to learn in a linear, one-step-at-a-time form. Everything is neat and in order. Television, on the other hand, is much more complex and rich. It develops in us a different "psychic environment." Moreover, this new psychic environment does not relate itself primarily to the conscious, logical levels of our mental operation. "The effects of technology do not occur at the level of opinions or concepts, but alter sense ratios or patterns of perception steadily and without any resistance."[2] It is not so much that we think differently about what we have received. Rather, we receive differently the materials about which we will later think. This changes everything.

The sermon based on neat, orderly, deductive logic, which is the kind of preaching that most of us have expected to hear, is derived from an age of writing. It was ideally suited to the way people used to learn. When the written word was supreme, the linear mode was primary. Letters were added to letters to make words. Words strung together made sentences, and sentences made paragraphs. All of it was arranged in orderly argument moving directly to conclusion. With electronic media it is much different: floods of impressions are presented, and there is often little apparent order except as it is supplied by the viewer's mind.[3]

The random presentation of images may be the most characteristic aspect of television. Typically there will be scenes here, scenes there, an instant here, an instant there, perhaps accompanied by flashbacks or flashes ahead, and the whole is broken at crucial moments by commercials. The overall effect is much more that of a montage than a book. There is no completeness, no unity except as the viewer's mind fits the pieces together and discovers its own completeness and unity.

This quality of being unfinished without the viewer's help is one of the factors which gives TV its sense of involvement with the audience. Television does not do everything for the viewer. The audience is left with a significant task: the people who watch must decide what the experience means.

There are many implications growing from this information. Let us at least notice that today's congregation, leaving its TV sets briefly to hear a sermon, will not have the patience to follow extended logical discourse that could have been expected a generation or two ago. In addition, the people who hear sermons today are used to being part of the action via TV. Many people will judge a message to be inappropriate, or at least uninteresting, if it is pre-chewed and predigested to the point that every argument is anticipated and every application complete.

The Speaking

The difficulties of speaking for God in an age of galloping change have driven many to reexamine the overall function of ministry in the light of the Scriptures. Today's pastor often sees the total leadership function—including preaching—to be that of an enabler. Taking a cue from the apostle Paul, the goal of the work is "to equip the saints for the work of ministry" (Ephesians

4:12). One who sees his or her responsibility in such a light is likely to be cautious about allowing the pulpit style to convey any suggestion of a dependent relationship like child to parent. One who hopes to set people free to exercise their own independent ministries can hardly be comfortable offering sermons in a manner which might imply that it is the pulpit's function to give answers and the people's function to receive them. Yet the very setting in which the person who preaches must function tends to make such a statement about the one who brings the message.

In *Moby Dick* Melville vividly describes the lofty pulpit in the whalemen's chapel at New Bedford. In order to enter it, the priest, Father Mapple, had to climb up a rope ladder. Having gained the security of his pulpit, he pulled the ladder up after himself, so that he was completely cut off from the congregation. Melville explains that it was an act symbolizing the complete self-sufficiency of that pulpit. Possessing God and the Scriptures in the security of that lofty eminence, the priest needed no one else.[4] Words spoken in such a setting would obviously carry the weight of great authority.

Such an extreme example of pulpit authority symbolized by church architecture would be hard to come by today, though some come close. Nevertheless, it is only the degree which has been modified in the typical worship setting of today. The basic sense of authority ascribed to the preaching function through the arrangement of church furniture has changed little. Most preaching is still done from pulpits. Most pulpits are still elevated above the level of the congregation. There are still clear understandings as to who is entitled to address the congregation from the pulpit when sermon time comes. Thus the preacher is likely to experience tension between his or her own inner sense of vocation and the physical setting in which the vocation must be practiced.

Nor is the tension reduced by the format of preaching. Customarily the preacher will do all the speaking. Everyone else is expected to attend regularly and listen. This has generally been understood to imply that the preacher is active while others are passive. The laity are thereby assigned a subordinate role. Understood this way, it is an arrangement which communicates a sense of dependence.[5]

Such a dependent relationship may even be enhanced by the organization of the sermon itself. Seminaries have often taught homiletics students to select a single key idea which they wish to convey, to announce it at the beginning, and to elaborate it and illustrate it in succeeding points within the message. Having been equipped with this model of sermon organization, it is possible to preach indefinitely without departing from the many variations of this style of organization which are available. This basic approach is both convenient and flexible and has much to commend it.

But notice what happens when the main point is given first and then broken down into smaller parts: the conclusion is placed ahead of the development. This is contrary to normal patterns of speech, except where it is assumed that the listeners will passively expect that the speaker is entitled to assert conclusions and make applications to the lives of those who hear.[6]

We are still only a few generations removed from those colonial times when the minister might well have been the only educated person in the village. Then the "parson" was the "person" indeed, and sermons which conveyed the note of confident authority from the very core of their organization were perfectly suited for the day.

But today is a different time. The modern preacher sees self, task, and people in a different light. Having undertaken to be one who equips the people for their own independent ministries, there is likely to be painful tension created within one's own person by returning weekly to a preaching format which seems to undercut the overall goals for ministry.

Any discussion of the preacher as a person should also recognize that this is a person under necessity. Some are eager to preach. Others would just as soon not, or at least not preach so often. Either way, preaching is not an option for most clergy, even though there may be times when they have more questions than answers. Most entered the pulpit in the first place out of a profound sense of being called to that particular vocation, and that call is still with them. They understand what Amos meant: "The lion has roared; who will not fear? The Lord GOD has spoken; who can but prophesy?" (Amos 3:8). They feel akin to Jeremiah: "If I say, 'I will not mention him, or speak any more in his name,' there is in my heart as it were a burning fire shut up in my bones, and I am weary with holding it in, and I cannot" (Jeremiah 20:9). So they preach, and they will keep on preaching. But many would like to find an approach to preaching more supportive of their overall goals for ministry.

The Words

In preaching, words are the link that bind preacher and hearer together. Perhaps it is not too fanciful to suggest that words, once spoken, may be thought of as having life of their own. In this sense words, too, are participants in the preaching act.

It is obvious that speaking is not going to cease, for it is the nature of human beings to communicate orally. Whether certain forms of oral communication will continue as they have in the past is another matter, which we now take up.

Apart from those who predict the death of preaching, we may observe that even some of the pulpit's best friends seem determined to convince us that the homiletical wave of the future lies with sermon forms which bear little resemblance to the preaching tradition which has come down to us. In such cases one is left feeling that this may be another example of successful surgery followed by the patient's death.

There is no intent here to disparage the experimental and the innovative. The bold, the fresh, and the unusual have their places. These are serious attempts to make the sermon less dependent upon linear modes of thought. Congregations and preachers alike may find a refreshing, invigorating change in leaving the familiar rut to share a fresh adventure together.

Nevertheless, it must not be assumed that nontraditional forms represent the shape of the future for the basic preaching format. Dialogue sermons, multimedia presentations, dramatic monologues, and chancel plays all have their places in the year's pulpit calendar. One hopes that every church will take advantage of what these methods offer. But it is probable that they neither should nor can replace the traditional sermon format, which has stood the test of time and remains as one of the basic means by which the church shares its faith. It is quite possible to preach inclusively within the traditional sermon style.

Critics who despair of the ability of the human voice, alone and unaided, to communicate the gospel effectively in an electronic age are overlooking the inherent power of the spoken word. Granted that our life is far different from that of our ancestors, yet we are still human. We are still in touch with our basic nature. So long as we are what we are, a word spoken aloud may affect us profoundly. Let us see how words participate with us in the event called preaching.

Fundamentally the value of preaching derives from human nature. We communicate with each other primarily through speech. Our Creator equipped us to produce identifiable oral sounds, to listen to those sounds, and to react. Speech is a uniquely human capability, an asset priceless beyond description and a solemn responsibility.

Since our thoughts are transmitted and our actions coordinated most basically through speech, this is the element most crucial to our ability to survive and function in society. The essential coordination of effort can only be accomplished through language.

Moreover, there is psychological evidence to indicate that the ability to hear, which is of course directly associated with the speaking function, is more fundamentally related to the kinds of persons we become than is true of our other senses. It seems that the congenitally deaf, if not properly helped, end up more intellectually retarded than the congenitally blind.[7] There is great strength in words!

Within this context, let us be aware of a pulpit concern. Reuel Howe cites a study of a thousand ministers from associated denominations and backgrounds, saying that all of them designated communication as their primary concern. "The chief source of their frustration was their sense of failing to open the lives of their people at any deep level to the meanings of the gospel." For their part, Howe stated, laymen point to a difference between the subject the words address and the feelings the words create within the listeners. For example, "the preacher's sermon . . . on the free gift of God's love is often heard by them simply as a new and harsher demand to be good."[8]

Such findings certainly support all that has been said before about the difficulties facing pulpit and pew. But let us note clearly that such examples only demonstrate that words are not being used effectively; they do not prove that words spoken aloud by one person and heard by others *cannot* be effective in opening lives to the gospel.

The spoken word has a capacity to create intimate relationships between persons that makes the written or printed word a poor substitute. Primitive people were so aware of the power of speech that they often exaggerated it to the point of superstition. Today the electronic media flourish on their ability to reproduce the voice as part of the overall impression which is offered.

Martin Buber spoke of the "I-Thou relationship" as the most powerful, most effective relationship between persons. This concept speaks of a way of being with others which continuously and consciously recognizes that you and I are here together, that we are each essential to the other, and that we must permit each to act upon the other. The point here is that the word spoken aloud has a unique capacity to create and sustain that sort of relationship between persons.

Oral speech encourages mutual awareness between persons and an open, trusting attitude because spoken words are by nature dialogical and inclusive. That is, what one says in conversation is not determined beforehand, but is largely shaped in response to what the other has already said. The concerns of each are included in the words chosen by the other.

Browne Barr has explored the power of the spoken word. In *The Well Church Book* he calls the church "an oral institution"and a "speech event."[9] Although the church has many symbols and forms of communication available to it, it is primarily the spoken word interchanged between persons that gives life and substance to the congregation of believers. Barr maintains that this is because "human speech may possess greater power than other forms of language to search out and reveal the interior of life, soul to soul, person to person, human and divine."[10]

His point is that speech is the most effective means by which one person may reveal his or her inner life to another. One may reveal strengthening faith or disabling doubt through the printed page or the graphic arts; skillfully done and properly utilized powerful communication may result. But Barr would insist that more powerful still is the self-revealing word by which one person may speak aloud for the hearing of another. It is the most directly personal and most self-revealing form of communication.

Indeed, Barr argues that words spoken aloud go beyond merely describing thoughts or circumstances to sharing in their actual creation. He has in mind that talking is a community event, requiring a minimum of two people. Wherever there is a community of persons the community creates speech, but speech also creates the community. That understanding leads to Barr's working definition of the church as it is expressed at the parish level: "The church is a group of people engaged in all kinds of conversation about Jesus of Nazareth and about a host of related persons and events."[11] For Barr, the experience by which a group of people find themselves to be the people of God is primarily oral—which would imply that preaching, proclaiming the words of faith aloud, is of the very essence of the church. Speaking the gospel calls the church into being.

In preaching, key elements of the church's life come together. Through words spoken aloud preacher and hearers may affect each other in ways both healing and life-changing, bringing a sense of the eternal to the temporal. The power is in the relationship created by the speaking.

Expectations of Change

Christian preaching has a note of the imperative about it. Preaching ordinarily is not done merely to inform, although informing may be a significant part of the preacher's goal. Persuading, urging, challenging, convicting, converting: these are words which belong to any standard definition of preaching. It is assumed that preaching produces change. We expect that change will occur when the gospel is preached. Yet the reality which is frequently experienced has been whimsically expressed by Halford Luccock, one of America's more famous preachers of a somewhat earlier time.

> I have been fascinated by the names of two little villages in Norfolk, in England, each of which has a parish church. The names are Great Snoring and Little Snoring. I have often felt as though I were the curate of the church at Little Snoring.[12]

Granted that changes, even significant changes, can and do occur inwardly without the knowledge of the preacher, there certainly are many among us who are convinced that they have experienced times when the word of preaching did in fact return void. It is possible to preach large numbers of sermons and see little by way of changed lives or circumstances to show for it. Considering that the aims of preaching are so directly stated in terms of change, it seems reasonable to expect that there should be some substantial results to which one might point. With so much cause around, there ought to be some effect!

Of course there really is. Testimonies to values received from sermons are readily available. Lives are changed. Conditions are altered. At times and places the kingdom of God does seem to come a bit closer because the Word has been preached.

But the proportion seems meager. It seems to take so much preaching to produce a bit of movement, and that proportion does not seem to match our expectations that preaching is a *powerful* agent for change. Discouragement is a predictable result, with a significant number of preachers eventually giving up in despair.

Fortunately that is not all that can be said about the results of preaching. The discouragement of some expresses a reality, but not necessarily the whole reality. If we are not satisfied with the degree of change resulting from our sermons, there are other avenues which we might wish to explore.

One such avenue which seems promising for making preaching more productive of change in life and events is the introduction of the prophetic element into our homiletical work. A prophetic stance in pulpit ministry clearly has a biblical base, and is generally regarded as an essential element of Christian preaching. The moral imperative that refuses to count the cost is the steel in the preacher's backbone; without it the efforts of the pulpit seem weak and flabby. But there are some considerations.

One is entitled to wonder what should be the format and style of prophetic preaching today. We can learn from the Bible how it was done by Jeremiah and Ezekiel, but it is left to our own creativity to decide how that translates to our own time and place.

In the 1960s there emerged a substantial number of clergy who understood the prophetic role as a call to direct interpersonal confrontation in word and deed. Civil rights and the Vietnam war, with its associated but only partly related opposition to the draft, were major issues. A militant spirit which many Americans had not encountered before seemed to be a dominant force in religious life. Certainly it captured the headlines.

During this period such militant activities occurred in a neighboring parish. The pastor there understood his role to be that of confronting his people so forcefully that they would be required to change their attitudes. During the week he traveled about the entire region to participate in whatever demonstrations were being organized. When there were none to be found, he organized some. The result was that week by week his people were confronted by newspaper accounts in which his name and their church were prominently mentioned. On one occasion there were pictures showing their pastor chained to a tree in the park to make it more difficult for the police to arrest him. On Sundays the confrontation became direct and personal, as he spoke from the pulpit to tell them bluntly that they were wrong and must change.

The pastor in this instance was sincere, courageous, and bold. There is no question that he was fulfilling with integrity the prophetic role as he understood it. Whether his approach was effective with respect to his congregation is another matter. His church grew rapidly smaller, and it was hard for him to see any material change in the opinions and attitudes of the people—except that they grew steadily more hostile toward their pastor. Eventually he concluded that his ministry no longer had a useful impact, so he resigned his parish and sought secular employment.

This pastor was only one of many who believed that confrontation is the only way to achieve social change. To be sure there are times when it seems necessary, but it is certainly not the only pulpit strategy. In view of its potential for creating fear and hostility, any use of direct confrontation in pastoral preaching must be carefully examined. If confrontation is seen as an end in itself, then we may feel justified in echoing the famous words "Damn the torpedoes. Full speed ahead!" But if the real goal of pulpit ministry is changed lives, it is appropriate to ask questions of strategy: What works? What is effective? What approaches are most likely to result in the desired change?

Dance and Larson examined the problem that faces any speaker who would attempt to influence an audience with strongly held opinions opposed to his or her own. They noted that a decision to confront may well be based on factors other than commitment to produce change. Their conclusion was that those who evangelically attempt to convert an audience's attitudes through direct opposition usually do so because the confrontation stance is more self-gratifying and more fun than other options! Under such conditions the results are likely to be other than those desired. The authors sound a strong warning.

> We advise you not to attempt major conversions in the attitudes of involved or highly committed audiences. Such attempts at major conversion, based on direct confrontation of opposing points of view, are likely to result in a rejection of you as a speaker and the further entrenchment of audience attitudes.[13]

A related dimension of the same issue emerges in studies of "assimilation-contrast effects." Such studies have demonstrated that a hearer's ability to receive a communication is affected by the hearer's commitment to a point of view. Persons highly committed to an opinion are likely to judge any other point of view as more divergent than it really is, increasing the likelihood of rejection. Persons with a low commitment to a point of view are likely to judge a differing opinion as less divergent than is really the case, thereby increasing the probability that the new opinion will be accepted.[14]

If "prophetic" is understood to be the application of God's Word to the human situation in the hope that persons may be caused to change, then findings such as these suggest that direct confrontation may be the least effective pulpit strategy. In the long run it may turn out to be more prophetic for the pulpit to concentrate on achieving a series of small changes rather than trying to cause a radical shift of attitude immediately. Initially the preaching might adopt a modest interim goal, perhaps merely asking hearers to be aware that there are other responsible people who have views different from their own. In time, through repetitive dealings with the matter, persons may be moved by small steps to the desired understanding.

There is, of course, some tension between modern secular wisdom and biblical example. It can scarcely be argued that Elijah, Jeremiah, and Amos adopted limited goals in their communication strategy. Their words were bold, blunt, and sometimes even brutal as they struggled to achieve major changes in the life of the nation. Preachers today must decide whether they can settle for less and still remain in the prophetic tradition.

In this connection it may be noted that the biblical prophets in general seem to have had little success in producing changes among those to whom their messages were most directly pointed. Nor is this surprising. A key element in Isaiah's prophetic call was that his preaching was to have the effect of confirming the people in their evil ways.

> And he said, "Go, and say to this people: 'Hear and hear, but do not understand; see and see, but do not perceive.' Make the heart of this people fat, and their ears heavy, and shut their eyes; lest they see with their eyes, and hear with their ears . . . and turn and be healed" (Isaiah 6:9-10).

Jeremiah and Ezekiel had similar elements in their own moments of calling to prophetic ministry (see Jeremiah 1:18-19; Ezekiel 2:4-5; 3:4-9). Evidently part of the prophetic role was to set the stage for judgment rather than change. It was not because of prophetic failure that King Ahab did not yield to Elijah and that Jeremiah's council was ignored. The hardening of hearts was part of the prophetic task.

This suggests that today's preachers who wish to stand in the prophetic stream must examine their goals closely. There may be times when firm, unrelenting witness to the Word which has come from God may be an end in itself. It may be that there is a valid ministry to "harden hearts" as a prelude to judgment. Nevertheless, to the extent that the prophetic strain in preaching has the changing of lives as its goal, the usefulness of direct pulpit confrontation would seem to be suspect.

Of course there are other examples of prophetic witness in the Bible, some of which were more productive of personal and societal change. The conversation between Nathan and King David has sometimes been cited as evidence that eyeball to eyeball confrontation is the biblically effective way (2 Samuel 12:1-15). However, Nathan was not engaged in public speaking; his was a personal conversation with the king. Nor was Nathan quite so direct as all that. He first told a parable; only after David judged himself through his reaction to the parable did Nathan make the application to David: "You are the man."

We may notice also that Nathan and his fellow prophets functioned within a social system in which they had an accepted role as spokesmen for God. In this capacity they sometimes acted as consultants to the government. Ahab, King of Israel, wanted Jehoshaphat, King of Judah, to assist him in capturing the territory of Ramoth-Gilead. Before Jehoshaphat would commit himself he needed assurance from the prophetic community that the Lord was favorable to this enterprise. Four hundred prophets encouraged the kings to proceed with their venture, but Micaiah withheld his support, saying that a "lying spirit" was using the other prophets to entice the kings into destruction. This minority report was upsetting to King Ahab, for it introduced an element of uncertainty into his personal project (1 Kings 22:1-18).

That lone dissenting prophetic voice which Micaiah represented was significant in light of the biblical belief that speaking the Word of God caused the predicted events to occur—a view which continued to be reflected throughout the New Testament. For instance, Matthew comments concerning the virgin birth of Jesus: "All this took place to fulfil what the Lord had spoken by the prophet . . ." (Matthew 1:22). In a similar vein Matthew later reports that Jesus spoke in parables because it had been predicted that he would do so:

> All this Jesus said to the crowds in parables; indeed he said nothing to them without a parable. This was to fulfil what was spoken by the prophet: "I will open my mouth in parables, I will utter what has been hidden since the foundation of the world" (Matthew 13:34-35).

This same belief in the power of the spoken prophetic word to bring reality into being is reflected in the words of the resurrected Christ, who indicated that his death was necessary because it had been predicted by the Law and the Prophets.

> Then [Jesus] said to [the disciples], "These are my words which I spoke to you, while I was still with you, that everything written about me in the law of Moses and the prophets and the psalms must be fulfilled." Then he opened their minds to understand the scriptures, and said to them, "Thus it is written, that the Christ should suffer and on the third day rise from the dead . . . (Luke 24:44-47).

This, of course, is much different from thinking of the prophets merely as having advance knowledge of future events. Here the spoken word was seen as a cause of Jesus' death and resurrection. In the same way Peter was convinced that the place among the company of disciples which Judas had held must be given to another because he found a prediction that it would be so (Acts 1:15-26).

When religious spokesmen were officially regarded as advisers to the government, and when kings believed that a prophetic word would produce its own reality, a message such as that brought by Nathan to King David could hardly be taken lightly. David's submission to Nathan is to his credit, but it is also in keeping with what might be expected of a pious ruler.

Today we live within an entirely different situation which calls for reexamination of our pulpit strategies. Too rigid an adherence to historic models of prophetic preaching may insure our failure to achieve the biblical goal. Perhaps there may be other models, equally biblical, more appropriate for today's needs. Such exploration is necessary if the expectation that changed lives and changed structures of society will follow the preaching of the Word of God is to become a reality.

Dialogic Style

Several aspects of the total pulpit presentation might be examined under "style." Shall one use many words, or adopt the more ascetic practice of brevity as a virtue? May colorful personality burst into bloom from the pulpit, or should a modest bearing be sought? Shall one use large words or small? Which is more effective, theological depth or emotional height? These and many other matters pertaining to the delivery of sermons add up to the particular style which any given preacher will claim as being just right for that person.

Among the many factors which make up the overall style with which preaching is done, there are some so fundamental that they shape choices concerning other less basic matters. One of these factors is the decision which each preacher and each congregation must make as to whether the sermon is primarily monologue or primarily dialogue. The choice that is made about this will influence such matters as subject, sermon organization and selection of words. It will affect tone of voice, and it may well help determine the overall structure of the worship service in which the sermon is preached. Whether the sermon is primarily monologue or dialogue is the matter of style to which we now turn.

"Monologue" and "dialogue" are words used to express varieties of meaning. In one context they refer simply to the number of persons speaking. If all the talking is being done by one person, it is monologue. If two or more persons are sharing the speaking and listening duties, the activity is called dialogue—especially if the exchanges are conversational in nature.

In another context the same two words may describe the manner of the speaking. One person may come before an assembly which remains silent while he speaks. Perceiving the listeners as an audience, this speaker relies heavily upon conclusions reached behind the closed doors of the study. The presentation addresses the speaker's concerns, questions and conclusions. When all is done, speaker and audience go their separate ways. Such an approach to the speaking task is rightly called monologue.

Another person may come before the same assembly, which will again remain silent while she speaks. This speaker perceives the people not so much as an audience, but rather as a group of colleagues from whom the speaker came and to whom the speaker will return. Conclusions reached behind the closed doors of the study may well be an important part of this presentation also, but this time the speaking will be substantially guided by the audience itself. The speaker has listened previously to the people, and the message addresses questions which they have asked and articulates concerns which they have voiced. The speaking concludes with a certain openendedness, for the speaker is aware that all will not have been said until the people have a chance to respond in the coming days. This approach to the speaking task is called dialogue, for it sees the oral presentation as but one phase of an extended conversation which began before the people gathered to hear the speaker and which continues after the speaker has finished.

When used in this sense, the words monologue and dialogue express different styles of relationship between speaker and hearer. Monologue deals primarily if not exclusively with the concerns and conclusions of the speaker, who attempts to persuade the audience to his or her way of thinking. Such a context for speaking contains at least the implication that the thoughts of the speaker are more important than those of the hearers. Dialogue, on the other hand, begins with the concerns of the gathered people. Their contribution to the speaking will be evident in subtle, if not overt ways. The speaker attempts to help the people think together, realizing that it is not necessary that they all come to the same opinion. The thoughts of those who listen are recognized as also having importance; they are included in the action.

Notice that the number of persons speaking and the manner in which they speak may occur in various combinations. One speaker (monologue) may address an audience in such a way that it is clear that this is part of a continuing conversation which began earlier and which will continue later (dialogue). In this instance the format is monological, but the style is dialogical.

On another occasion several persons may share the platform, taking turns speaking and perhaps pausing for the audience to make comments or ask questions. This is a dialogical format, and if they are truly listening and responding to one another, the style is dialogical also. If, however, they are merely waiting for one another to stop talking in order to have a chance to make the statement that each one believes is *really* important, then the style is monological.

The format of Christian preaching has traditionally been monological and the assumption here is that this will continue to be true in the majority of instances. Preaching will usually be done by a single individual who speaks while others listen. The concern we are addressing is whether the *style* of preaching should be monological or dialogical.

Numerous persons have dealt with this issue in print, though some have not used this particular terminology. For instance, Clement Welsh has commented on the tendencies of some preachers to attempt to impose their views on their congregations.

> Preaching has strong overtones of being an adversary action, given by the authoritative person of the preacher and the very place and structure of the pulpit a dictatorial quality which is either resented by the strong or unfortunately cherished by the weak. But the preacher should not preach like a lord chancellor. Preaching is essentially a pastoral action. Like pastoral counseling, it is intended to help the person to discover the gospel for himself, and to make it his own, and the obedient acceptance of an imposed faith is simply destructive of that possibility.[15]

Some popular preachers of the past and present have exhibited the tendencies which Welsh criticizes. This is clearly seen in "Songs in the Night," a sermon preached by Charles Haddon Spurgeon in his younger years. In this sermon Spurgeon said:

> Religion is not a thing merely for your intellect; a thing to prove your own talent upon, by making a syllogism on it; it is a thing that demands your faith. As a messenger of heaven, I demand that faith;

if you do not choose to give it, on your own head be the doom, if there be such; if there be not, you are prepared to risk it. But I have done my duty; I have told you the truth; that is enough, and there I leave it.[16]

Not much room for conversation there! The listener is expected to respond as the preacher requires; if that response is withheld, then the preacher washes his hands of the whole relationship. Such a style is clearly monological.

Billy Graham is generally conceded to be the most listened-to preacher in America today, and perhaps in the world. The same note of imposed authority may be observed in his preaching, as, for instance, in a sermon called "Why God Allows Suffering and War."

What do you have to do? You have to respond to God's offer of forgiveness and love and mercy. There are thousands of people in Houston who belong to a church who have never really done that. You have your name on a church roll but God is not looking at that. You live a good decent life but that is not good enough. You have to have a personal relationship with Christ. There are three things you have to do. . . .[17]

This is not a style of people reasoning together. The speaker is attempting to overcome what he perceives as perhaps spiritual inertia; the congregation is being told what it is to think and what it is to do. Again, this is monological. Some highly popular preachers choose to work in this way.

Is monologue appropriate for an average pastor in an average parish? That is a different matter. Spurgeon spoke to a much earlier generation under conditions markedly different from those of today. Billy Graham speaks to mass audiences gathered specifically for an evangelistic event, with both preacher and congregation knowing that they will be together for but a few sermons at most, and with small likelihood that there will be a continuing relationship on any level. The parish pastor preaches under a different set of circumstances, which may well call forth a different method. Again, each must decide what is most appropriate.

It is instructive, however, to recall the visit of Pope John Paul II to America. Great crowds turned out to hear him wherever he went, expressing great appreciation and warmth for one who is widely perceived as a genuine man of God, even by non-Roman Catholics. In this context of immense goodwill and readiness to hear what he might have to say, the Pope took occasion to reaffirm his church's historic stands on such issues as celibacy, male clergy, abortion, and birth control. These statements were based on the platform of papal authority, basically telling the people why they ought to do as their church commanded, without addressing the concerns which have prompted so many Roman Catholics to deviate from the historic practices of their faith. The reaction of many has been that the Pope is a good man whom they admire greatly, but the laity also see themselves as fully capable of moral judgment and they will do as they please in sensitive areas. That is a predictable response to preaching which does not take into account the thoughts and concerns of the people to whom it is addressed.

Reuel Howe is one of the most widely known proponents of the dialogical, not only with respect to preaching but with respect to all communication. It is appropriate to report his opinion at some length.

Howe's point of view is that preaching is commonly a one-way event, and that this characteristic is in opposition to any hope that communication may occur through the sermon event. Communication is intended to bring together meanings from both sides, but monologue is really only interested in imposing meaning from one side. A predictable result is that people tend to be removed from active participation in the sermon, with a corresponding loss of relevance for the hearers. The clergy assume a monopolistic role. One speaks while others can only listen. The whole event may seem distant and impersonal. There is little incentive to struggle to find the meaning of the Word for today, resulting in a loss of power.[18]

Moreover, commitment to a monological style may be said to have a "snowball" effect as far as the preacher's isolation from the people is concerned. The end result is that the preacher is increasingly in a position of arrogance with respect to the congregation. Since the sole commitment is to speaking, the monological preacher neither sees nor hears. If there begins to be a suspicion that the speaking is not going well, anxiety about that will produce still more speaking and still less seeing and hearing. At the extreme, Howe believes, it may almost be said that one who preaches monologically possesses the Word and that there is no other channel through which God may speak.[19]

That is a position which one might wish to debate. At least it may be said that it represents an extreme position which would not necessarily be wholly true concerning all preachers whose style is basically monological. Yet the fact remains: The more a preacher's talking prevents his or her own seeing and hearing, the more likely that person is to have difficulty communicating. Howe is utterly pessimistic about the values to be obtained from preaching which is monological in style.

> [Another] characteristic of conventional preaching is seen in the absence of organized response or feedback from the congregation. Lack of feedback strengthens all the stereotypes which people entertain about preaching. Preaching is frequently done to an invisible congregation because the lights have been turned down; yet the facial expressions and bodily postures and movements of the congregation are communications in response to the preacher, and he needs to see and note them as at least partial guidance for his speaking. The custom of preaching without response from the congregation is irresponsible communication and endangers, more than anything else, the preacher's relevance.[20]

Howe believes that a "crisis of preaching" exists because of a general use of the monological style. Lack of intercommunication between pulpit and pew means that neither can accurately understand the other, so that the Word of preaching fails to touch the hearers at the point of their need. The meanings of the gospel do not touch the meanings we bring from our lives. The urgent questions which arise out of our living miss contact with the timeless truths of God's Word. Howe concludes that monological, clergy-centered preaching simply does not have the capacity to bring God and man together in healing ways.[21]

In his earlier book, *The Miracle of Dialogue,* Howe suggested four purposes for communication which are of particular relevance for preaching.

> 1. Communication is a means by which information and meaning is conveyed and received between individuals and groups. . . .
> 2. A second purpose of communication is to help persons make a responsible decision [respects a responsible "no"—helps people see consequences of choices]. . . .
> 3. Another purpose of communication . . . is to bring back the forms of life into relation to the vitality which originally produced them. . . .
> 4. A final purpose of dialogue is to bring persons into being. Man becomes man in personal encounter, but personal encounter requires address and response between person and person. . . .[22]

Howe's contention is that dialogue, and only dialogue, has the capacity to produce that sort of communication. If he and others who agree with him are correct, it would seem that dialogical style is a most appropriate response to concerns about pulpit authority and expectations of change, for it removes barriers which hinder effective proclamation of the gospel through preaching.

CHAPTER 2

Biblical and Theological Roots

Christianity is a revealed religion. From beginning to end the Bible states that human wisdom does not search out and expose the secrets that God would prefer to keep hidden. Humankind knows only those things which God has chosen to disclose, no more and no less. Whether we are speaking of Adam at the beginning or St. John the Divine at the ending, the Scriptures record that which the sovereign activity of God has made known.

It is equally clear that profound changes occur in human life when a person is in direct contact with the Living God. People do not pass through moments of revelation while remaining as they were; to know God is to be changed. The power which accomplishes this, however, is not in the knowledge which is given, important though that may be. The power is in the relationship established. Being in the presence of God alters life forever. It is, in fact, the necessary element. Intellectual understanding is not enough, nor is it necessarily essential.

Preaching which has the capacity to change lives, then, is linked to revelation in the closest possible way. It is to the relationship between the two that we now turn.

The Dialogical Nature of Revelation

A shepherd was leading his flock on the edge of an ancient wilderness when he observed a remarkable circumstance: a bush was burning, but it was not being consumed. Obeying his natural curiosity, the shepherd moved closer to find out how this could be. He heard his name being called and he responded. That was when he discovered that he had come into the presence of God, and that God had a surprising task for him.

> Then the LORD said, "I have seen the affliction of my people who are in Egypt, and have heard their cry because of their taskmasters;

> I know their sufferings, and I have come down to deliver them out
> of the hand of the Egyptians, and to bring them up out of that land
> to a good and broad land, a land flowing with milk and honey. . . .
> Come, I will send you to Pharaoh that you may bring forth my
> people, the sons of Israel, out of Egypt" (Exodus 3:7-10).

This was the beginning of an extended conversation between
God and a most reluctant servant. Whether Moses held back out
of unwillingness to put himself at God's disposal or out of modest
inability to think of himself as qualified for such a task is not
known. What is known is that Moses asked penetrating questions
of God and offered excellent reasons why he felt that he was a poor
choice. God answered each objection in turn until Moses was finally
willing to gather up his family and make his way back to Egypt.

In this conversation may be seen a consistent characteristic of
the self-disclosures of God: revelation is dialogical. The events or
encounters in which the Word makes itself known both permit and
require a response.

In another encounter Ezekiel found himself called through a
vision to a prophetic ministry. Undoubtedly Ezekiel would have
wanted to speak comforting words to his fellow exiles, words
which would effectively rally them back to the Lord so that their
Babylonian slavery might quickly end. Unfortunately for him the
vision of his calling made it clear that his ministry was to be among
a rebellious people who would refuse to pay attention. The effect
of his speaking, therefore, would be to confirm them in their
rebellion against God and thus lengthen the time of their servitude.
His response to this heartbreaking news was to avoid preaching
for a time. He needed to be alone with his thoughts. Describing
the experience later, Ezekiel felt supported by God in his need.

> The Spirit lifted me up and took me away, and I went in bitterness
> in the heat of my spirit, the hand of the LORD being strong upon me;
> and I came to the exiles at Telabib, who dwelt by the river Chebar.
> And I sat there overwhelmed among them seven days (Ezekiel 3:14-
> 15).

The entry of the divine Word into the world in the person of
Jesus was, of course, the revelation event *par excellence*. People who
met him with their minds open to any degree came away with a
new perception of God and themselves in relation to God. His style
was conversational, encouraging questions and debate. With great
skill he drew out of people insights that they never expected to find
within themselves, as for instance when Peter surprised himself
with the discovery that he was prepared to bestow on Jesus the

revered title "Christ," or when an unnamed woman at a Samaritan well discovered spiritual longings that she had not known she possessed.

The dealings which Jesus had with people were consistently invitational rather than forced. He would not heal without first seeing whether healing was desired. Those whom he invited to follow him were free to leave their usual business and come along, but they were equally free to decline the invitation.

> And behold, one came up to him, saying, "Teacher, what good deed must I do, to have eternal life?". . . . Jesus said to him, "If you would be perfect, go, sell what you possess and give to the poor, and you will have treasure in heaven; and come, follow me." When the young man heard this he went away sorrowful; for he had great possessions (Matthew 19:16-22).

The same dialogical style occurs throughout the New Testament. Wherever God discloses himself to a person, there is both opportunity and necessity for the one who is face to face with God to make a response of his or her own choosing. When the risen Christ appeared to Saul on the road to Damascus, Saul asked a question ("Who are you, Lord?") and received an answer ("I am Jesus, whom you are persecuting"). Even in the drama of the revelation granted to John, when John found himself spiritually transported to heaven, he was engaged in dialogue! Indeed, the vision involved John in direct participation at various times, as when he was given a measuring rod and told to go measure the temple (Revelation 11:1).

Perhaps, though, it is in the parables of Jesus that we see most clearly the extent to which God's self-disclosing acts of revelation are dialogical.

> "The kingdom of heaven is like a grain of mustard seed which a man took and sowed in his field; it is the smallest of all seeds, but when it has grown it is the greatest of shrubs and becomes a tree, so that the birds of the air come and make nests in its branches" (Matthew 13:31-32).

The parable is incomplete. No application is provided, no interpretation. What is the meaning of the parable? There is none given. The hearer must supply the meaning. A partnership is sought between the teller and the hearer. If the one who hears will enter into the partnership and complete the story, the story will have meaning; if the hearer refuses to participate, the story will remain meaningless.

The same thing may be observed with respect to other parables.

"The kingdom of heaven is like leaven which a woman took and hid in three measures of flour, till it was all leavened" (Matthew 13:33). It is as though God creates the condition in which revelation may be received through the mind of Christ, but relies upon the mind of the hearer actually to bring forth the crucial insight.

The bringing forth of insight out of the mind of the hearer is not necessarily a simple process to be completed at the instant of hearing. David M. Granskou speaks of "dialectic" in connection with parables, observing that "Parable . . . provides a springboard for reflection. It functions to turn people on, to unwrap truth (rather than to wrap it up), to cause wonder and laughter."[1] Parable, then, may well involve the hearer in extended inner debate with the outcome long in doubt and the final perception of truth long delayed. It is a lively, vital process which can never happen at all unless the one to whom the parable is given also participates.

At an even deeper, more complex level it may be observed that at least some of the parables cause their hearers to judge themselves. The judgment is not an external verdict imposed by an outside authority; it is rather that the hearer's own reaction to the story becomes a kind of internal judgment.

For instance, the Parable of the Loving Father—more commonly called the Parable of the Prodigal Son—may produce a variety of reactions, depending upon with which character one identifies (Luke 15:11-32). A parent who has had wayward children in the family may identify with the father in the story. Depending upon whether the parent's own behavior is confirmed or challenged by the father in the story, such a person may be left with joy or rage at the end of the story. Another may identify with the wandering son, experiencing vicariously the welcome relief of a warm homecoming. Still another may relate to the older brother, saying angrily at the end, "It isn't fair." Any of these reactions constitutes a form of inner self-judgment. God's position in the story is crystal clear: the father extends himself lovingly toward *both* sons. The hearer knows instinctively whether his or her inner reaction conforms to the standard of God's mercy.

Other parables have the same power to cause the hearer to bring forth a self-judging reaction. Particularly notable is the Parable of the Generous Employer (Matthew 20:1-16). An adult Sunday school class was discussing this parable one day when it became apparent that the group was sharply divided. Several thought it one of the most beautiful of all the sayings of Jesus, illuminating in a particularly clear way the generosity of a God who graciously gives far more than his people can ever deserve. Others became angry, feeling that God was here pictured as unjust and arbitrary. One woman in particular voiced bitterness, refusing to believe that the story could have come from Jesus. After extended discussion most of the class agreed that the gospel is not Good News to everyone; some people are not yet prepared to accept the kind of God revealed through Jesus Christ. Such is the inner judgment which some of the parables provoke.

It might reasonably be expected that anyone who tells stories which bring the hearers eyeball-to-eyeball with their own good and evil selves would end up in the center of controversy. That, of course, is exactly what happened to Jesus. Joachim Jeremias has spelled that out for us.

> The parables of Jesus are not—at any rate primarily—literary productions, nor is it their object to lay down general maxims ('no one would crucify a teacher who told pleasant stories to enforce prudential morality'), but each of them was uttered in an actual situation of the life of Jesus, at a particular and often unforeseen point. Moreover . . . they were preponderantly concerned with a situation of conflict. They correct, reprove, attack. For the greater part, though not exclusively, the parables are weapons of warfare. Every one of them calls for immediate response.[2]

The dialogical nature of parables is consistent with the larger pattern of Scripture as a whole. Different parts of the Bible offer differing perceptions of God and his message to his people. The Bible does not offer a single, monolithic point of view. Many kinds of debates are carried on within the pages of Scripture.

This characteristic of the Bible automatically requires that any reader who attempts to deal with the sacred writings comprehensively rather than verse by verse also must be in dialogue with the Scriptures. Serious conversation between book and reader is essential for understanding the broad sweep of the biblical material.

Does Isaiah's prophecy offer hope for the people of Israel? "Very little," one might say. "Israel's prospects are grim."

> Zion shall be redeemed by justice, and those in her who repent, by righteousness. But rebels and sinners shall be destroyed together, and those who forsake the LORD shall be consumed. . . . For you shall be like an oak whose leaf withers, and like a garden without water. And the strong shall become tow, and his work a spark, and both of them shall burn together, with none to quench them (Isaiah 1:27-31).

But another reader may say, "Hold on. Isaiah has great hope for Israel. There are tender, lovely promises." And so there are.

Comfort, comfort my people, says your God. Speak tenderly to Jerusalem, and cry to her that her warfare is ended, that her iniquity is pardoned, that she has received from the LORD'S hand double for all her sins (Isaiah 40:1-2).

Which of these contradictory prophecies is Word of God to us? Both are! Which may we conveniently overlook? Neither! The responsible reader must enter into dialogue and decide where the balance lies between hopelessness and hope. The reader who pursues the history of Scripture discovers that what we receive as a single book called *Isaiah* was written by several people who did their work many years apart, so that both points of view could be appropriate to Israel at different times in history. Such an insight, however, is unlikely to be gained except through serious struggle between book and reader.

Does salvation come by works or by faith? Varieties of answers are possible, depending upon whether one reads James or Romans—or, indeed, which part of Romans. The one who reads them both in their entirety will not have as simple an answer as the person who reads only part of either.

Is God a righteous judge or a forgiving father? It depends upon whether one reads the Old Testament or the New Testament, or which parts of the New Testament one examines. Probably most thoughful readers of Scripture will affirm that God is both, but still there will be major disagreements as to which role is dominant within the personhood of God. Such debate is entirely appropriate, for the Bible is not long on black-and-white answers. It offers diverse points of view that engage the reader in dialogue.

James Smart has observed that many persons do not expect to enter into this kind of dialogical relationship with Scripture, preferring instead a more passive stance. He has sharply challenged the appropriateness of merely hearing and receiving Scripture. Smart asserts that passive "respectful" listening may not be listening at all. Hearing that does not ask questions and demand answers is not worthy of the name. He observes that the Hebrew verb for "hear" implies the response of the entire person.

For Smart the assumption that one is free to deal in a passive, nonreactive way with the Bible suggests a failure to recognize that God himself approaches us through the written word.

The sheer passivity which is so widely assumed to be an expression of respect for the Bible is exposed as hypocrisy as soon as a man comes into firsthand encounter with the word to which the biblical records bear witness. The word of God is God in his word addressing man, and in addressing him . . . claiming him in love for fellowship with himself, making him know his blindness and at the same time giving him sight. In this encounter no man can remain passive or silent.[3]

If we are thus meeting God through Scripture in a direct, intensely personal way, one may suppose that there would be the same sort of dialogical, life-changing encounter that is reported over and over again in the Bible. Smart affirms that this is exactly what one ought to look for, proposing that such a sense of direct encounter is the appropriate standard by which the adequacy of scriptural interpretations may be measured.[4]

Such a view of the Word in Scripture is consistent with the experience that we have whenever and wherever the Word meets us directly in life. The church gladly affirms that God still speaks directly with his people from time to time in moments of spiritual insight. These are times of excitement and wonder as a person says, "Aha! Now I see."

Such moments do not occur in splendid isolation from the stream of life. They are part of life, and are given as we participate in specific, tangible events which can be precisely identified as to time, date, and location. It is never something that happens in sterile objectivity. Rather we experience God being with us, sharing whatever event engages us at the moment and transforming it— and us—by his presence.

The "withness" of such an experience of God and man recognizing each other guarantees that it is a participatory event. No one encountering God directly can be merely a spectator. The gospel involves us as actors in the continuing creation which God and man do together.

> The Gospel, then, is not a self-contained entity out there or back there which is narrated in its purity for ten minutes, with a final ten minutes devoted to milking lessons from it for us today. Those who hear are not just an audience; they are participants in the story. The pure Gospel has fingerprints all over it. Recall how Paul understood the cross in the light of his suffering and understood his suffering in the light of the cross.[5]

We affirm, therefore, that the "Aha!" moments when we discover God acting directly within our lives are dialogical. They include us with all of our hopes and fears. Drawing us into the action, they both permit and require a response from the persons to whom they come. That is the way God has acted in the past. That is the way we experience him today.

Adoniram Judson, the pioneer American missionary to Burma, passed through a long inner struggle before he reached a sense of being confronted with the mind of Christ. Once that "Aha!" moment occurred, however, he immediately felt the necessity of decision.

Burma was much in Adoniram's thought. . . .

> He debated the problem with himself all through that fall of 1809. Christmas passed, and the New Year came. . . . Then one day in February . . . a message came to him while he was walking in the grove. . . . He never recorded the day or the time of day. We know only that "It was during a solitary walk in the woods behind the college, while meditating and praying on the subject, and feeling half inclined to give it up, that the command of Christ, 'Go into all the world and preach the Gospel to every creature,' was presented to my mind with such clearness and power, that I came to a full decision, and though great difficulties appeared in my way, resolved to obey the command at all events."[6]

We remember, though, that the conversation between God and an individual is so free and unforced that the person is as free to say "no" to God as to say "yes." That is the very evidence that the dialogue is genuine. When God comes to us we are treated with such respect that we are at all times able to refuse whatever insight or invitation may be put before us.

Keith Miller has graphically described a time when he and his wife had become so hostile toward each other that their marriage was in danger. As the situation unfolded, it became perfectly clear to him what God wanted him to do. The mind of Christ was that he should apologize and confess his share of responsibility for the problem.

> But when I looked over and cleared my throat, *I could not do it.* "I'll confess later," I thought to myself. But, for the first time in years, I could not. I went to bed filled with resentment. As I lay there in the dark, blinking back tears of rage and frustration, I realized again that I was a helpless little boy who not only could not do what he knew was right, but didn't want to. There was no solution.[7]

The following day Keith Miller shared his problem with Christian friends who helped him see that the key point was that he did not want to do what he knew God wanted; he preferred his pride to the will of God.

The dialogue which we have with God in life is so genuine that we may make any response which we choose. The only thing we cannot do is to meet God and make no response at all.

Preaching as a Revelation Event

The prophet Ezekiel offers a graphic representation of what may be accomplished through preaching.

> The hand of the LORD was upon me, and he brought me out by the Spirit of the LORD, and set me down in the midst of the valley; it was full of bones. And he led me round among them; and behold, there were very many upon the valley; and lo, they were very dry. And he said to me, "Son of man, can these bones live?" And I answered, "O Lord GOD, thou knowest." Again he said to me, "Prophesy to these bones, and say to them, O dry bones, hear the word of the LORD. Thus says the Lord GOD to these bones: Behold, I will cause breath to enter you, and you shall live. And I will lay sinews upon you, and will cause flesh to come upon you, and cover you with skin, and put breath in you, and you shall live; and you shall know that I am the LORD."
>
> So I prophesied as I was commanded; and as I prophesied there was a noise, and behold, a rattling; and the bones came together, bone to its bone. And as I looked, there were sinews on them . . . and skin had covered them; but there was no breath in them. Then he said to me, "Prophesy to the breath, prophesy, son of man, and say to the breath, Thus says the Lord GOD: Come from the four winds, O breath, and breathe upon these slain, that they may live." So I prophesied as he commanded me, and the breath came into them, and they lived, and stood upon their feet, an exceedingly great host (Ezekiel 37:1-10).

Here, in the vivid language of the prophetic vision, is set before us the end result of the proclamation of the Word: those who seem hopelessly dead are given new life by the power of God. The gift of life is given in conjunction with the proclaiming activity of the one who stands forth to say, "Thus says the Lord." But the source of that gift of life is not in doubt for a moment. God, not the preacher, gives life.

John Killinger has expressed in more contemporary terms the effects which the gift of life through preaching causes today.

> I have seen a few preachers. . . . whose preaching galvanizes men— upends them, probes them, haunts them, follows them into their most remote hiding places and smokes them out, drives them out coughing and sputtering and crying into the open light of new grace and new freedom and new love. The withered are made whole, and the lame leap for joy, the dumb find articulation, the confused direction, the harried find resources for slowing down.[8]

Both prophet and professor picture preaching as a salvation event in which God discloses himself and his purposes to needy people. This invites some observations about preaching.

Preaching is one of the sovereign activities of God. It would be a major mistake to suppose preaching originates with the preacher. Just as Ezekiel did not speak to the dry bones on his own initiative, but rather dared to obey the divine command, so does today's preacher if he or she is true to the commission which has been received. If the precise way that God expresses himself through the pulpit is difficult to describe, it may be remembered that none of God's actions fits easily into human words.

Karl Barth has admitted the difficulty which the theologian has in adequately describing what happens during preaching. Nevertheless, Barth finds no confusion or uncertainty about the ultimate origins of the preaching act. God is determined to make himself known. Preaching is an act of obedience on the part of human beings who have listened to the will of God. It is the human response to a divine command.[9]

Others bear witness to the same theme, that it is God who is active in the preaching event. In a particularly helpful way Killinger has caught a perspective which illuminates the relationship between God's sovereign activity in preaching and other activities of God recorded in the Bible.

> Imagine now: sermons . . . are actually pieces of revelation—just as good poems and paintings and sonatas are. Only, as the preacher lives constantly closer to the dreaded center of life's meaning, it is to be expected that the revelation in his work will plummet faster and surer and more breath-takingly to the heart of any matter.[10]

No matter what the time or place, all revelation has this in common: it is God's voluntary self-disclosure; it is breathtaking and life-changing wherever and whenever God chooses to make himself known. We dare to believe that we may create conditions under which persons are more open to perceive the activity of God, but God alone chooses when and where and to whom he will appear.

It may also be observed that preaching is not an activity of the church. Rather, it is an expression of the church. Where the church is being itself, there is preaching. Were it otherwise—that is, were preaching merely an activity of the church—then it would be one activity among many. As such, it would be optional, for no congregation can do everything, and choices must be made. But the spoken proclamation of the gospel is an essential expression of what the church is. Wherever the church exists there will be preaching, for it is one of the mighty acts by which God discloses himself.

The church should not concern itself with whether or not there will be preaching. It can and does ask how the preaching will best be accomplished. Questions of form, style, and content are ever with us, and rightly so. The unchanging gospel always requires expressions suited to a constantly changing world, so critique and analysis of the preaching task are forever appropriate. But it is as futile for the church to ask whether there will be burning where there is a fire as to ask whether there will be preaching.

A final observation is that the revelation given through preaching has salvation as its purpose. Of course it is true that any given sermon may serve several functions. One may quite properly look to the pulpit as a medium of education, for instance. But anything apart from salvation is subsidiary. Preaching falls short of its intended purpose unless it becomes a significant moment in which some portion of broken life is made whole by the grace of God.

The salvation given in the encounter between God and persons which is facilitated through preaching has a once-for-allness about it. There is a sense in which one sermon is enough for a lifetime: the responsive hearer is from that moment in Christ. Each sermon, then, potentially carries with it the touch of eternity.

At the same time those who have already been saved continue to need to be saved. That is, there is a continuing work of perfecting or sanctification to be accomplished. Many more meetings with God will be necessary before the person can approach Christian maturity in the likeness of Jesus Christ. Indeed, it will absorb a lifetime, and still the work will not be fully done. The preaching of the gospel needs to be heard many times over as one of the primary ways in which God's continuing revelation of himself to growing Christians occurs. This is one of the ways in which the work of salvation continues in the life of each hearer.

The salvation of persons through preaching is facilitated through the personal relationship which preaching establishes. God is not content that creature and Creator observe each other remotely at a distance. The person who is saved through Jesus Christ enters into a personal encounter of the most intimate nature. Throughout the ages of redemptive history, preaching has facilitated that relationship. The sermon does not merely address a crowd; it comes to individual persons to challenge, to probe, to bring hope, to demand a decision. It is the medium of a divine conversation which is extremely personal in its effect.

That kind of personal encounter is a function for which the oral proclamation is particularly well adapted. Words offered aloud, warm with life and vibrant with urgency, have a capacity to evoke response which other forms of communication do not possess in the same degree. A total relationship develops between speaker and hearer which is most especially suited for the conveying of an urgent message. Nothing of print or electronics is as effective in developing the directly personal encounter which is so much a part of Christian preaching.

In this connection there is another important consideration concerning the saving activity of God as it takes place through preaching. It is not to be suggested that the preacher who has "arrived" offers to set right those who are less fortunate or less advanced. Rather the salvation inherent in the preaching event runs to needy people on both sides of the pulpit. Indeed, this is a measure of its authenticity, that it gives life simultaneously to those who speak and those who hear.

> Not only the most dangerous, but above all the most wonderful, thing which can happen among men is that human beings in all their disobedience and ignorance can be used to preach the good news of God in Christ. Men can speak the Word of life. Their witness can change hearts and create lives. The Word of the living Lord can really be heard in the sermon: "I who speak to you am he." (John 4:26). . . . The preacher himself will be cleansed and forgiven. He himself will be a new man. He will not preach because he is a new man— what would happen if we wanted to rely on this?—but the very sermon he preaches will make him a new creation, just as it gives the bread of life to the congregation.[11]

When Paul spoke of the sermon as an instrument of salvation, he was not merely indulging in "preacher talk." He was stating the essential nature of preaching when he said, "For since, in the wisdom of God, the world did not know God through wisdom, it pleased God through the folly of what we preach to save those who believe" (I Corinthians 1:21). The revelation which comes through preaching has salvation as its purpose; anything short of that vision produces something less than preaching.

Although preaching can and does serve a number of subsidiary functions, its primary and essential purpose is to bring healing restoration to the broken relationship between God and humanity again and again, as many times as necessary. The preaching of the gospel is an act done at the initiative of God. It provides a particular setting wherein God and people find themselves face to face. When that happens, people cannot help but make a response, though each person decides what the response will be. Preaching, when it is used of God, is always dialogical at its core, no matter what the surface form may be.

This is, of course, a description of preaching as a revelation event. The preacher's aim can never be merely to inform. The preacher seeks to create a memorable occasion in which people find that they have come into the presence of the Living God.

Such a purpose cannot help but affect pulpit strategy. Since preaching at its core is always dialogical, it is helpful to look more closely at the creative partnership which must exist between pulpit and pew so that we can better understand what it is that our sermons need to accomplish. Then we can plan our preaching strategies accordingly.

CHAPTER 3

Preaching Dialogically

Preaching can be a lonely business. It is quite possible to approach the pulpit ministry in such a way as to magnify a sense of isolation between pastor and people. The contention of this chapter, however, is that such loneliness need not be accepted as mandatory. Let us rather take this as our vision: preaching is a function shared jointly between congregation and preacher.

Preaching as a Function of the Whole Church

No matter what other considerations might be involved, the Protestant understanding of the church does not permit the preacher to handle the gospel alone. At the core of the Reformation was the conviction that the laity are able to think for themselves and are indeed obligated to do so. Preachers are required to aid this thoughtful process. Clergy may exercise their utmost powers of persuasion, but tradition prohibits any attempt to exercise the powers of a dictator. People cannot be required to believe anything on the preacher's authority.

In other words, no matter what expectations may be in the preacher's mind, the Protestant congregation is going to take the sermon and do with it what it will. Meanings will be added and subtracted. Propositions will be approved, disapproved, and altered altogether. Assumptions will be affirmed or denied; conclusions will be supported, contradicted, or ignored.

Reuel Howe has observed that the sermon delivered on any given occasion really consists of many sermons: the sermon which was spoken aloud by the preacher; the sermon which was heard by each individual hearer; and the combined effect of all of these. Together, all of these constitute the church's sermon for that occasion.[1] In short, preaching is a congregational function.

Several practical as well as theological reasons support this understanding. One is the basic observation that speaking is affected by hearing. How well one listens has its effect on what is said. Those who listen well find that others do surprisingly well at communicating thoughts and information in an interesting, relevant manner. Others who listen with only half their attention seldom hear a good speaker.

Said another way, any message reflects to some degree the attitudes of those who hear it. If the congregation is intent, responsive, enthusiastic, and supportive, it will have a bearing on the delivery and the choice of words used by the preacher. If the congregation is of the opposite sort, that too will show up in the message.

The whole communication process operates in subtle but profound ways to guarantee that the hearer will have a hand in shaping the message, at least as it is received. In any sort of extended discourse the tendency is for the hearer to pick up a single fragment of thought which seems particularly important to that person. While the speaker continues on, the hearer lingers behind to caress an idea which has captured the imagination. This may be a helping, healing, satisfying time. The opposite can also be true if the hearer has been caught by a thought which is in opposition to that person's values. Either way, these are the important parts of the message for the hearer, though the speaker may have intended something quite different.

The natural extension of that process is that the hearer attributes her or his own thoughts to the speaker. Depending upon what those thoughts are, the preacher may or may not be pleased to receive the credit! Nevertheless, it goes on all the time; no doubt every preacher has received thanks or blame for some comment which was not in the sermon at all. This is a primary way each member of the congregation can add personal meaning to the preaching.

A variation on the same theme comes with the recognition that words—the basic building blocks of communication—are slippery. Every individual assigns a unique set of meanings to each and every word. In this way we "possess" words and make them our own. It also guarantees that what you say will, to me, mean what I decide it means.

This is a matter with which all communicators in all fields must cope, since it is inherent in language itself. A writer concerned with technical information related this incident.

After questioning one of my students recently as to what he meant by the term "reasonably sure," I received this amusing explanation: "'Sure' conveys no information by itself. It serves merely as a convenient point from which to express varying degrees of certainty. Each expression has a special significance to the engineer." He then wrote the following list on the board:

> Not quite sure
> Fairly sure
> Rather sure
> Reasonably sure
> SURE
> Very sure
> Real sure
> Sure indeed
> Sure as hell[2]

Behind this anecdote is a cold reality. Communication is an intimate, subjective act. Words are not carved in granite to be passed from one to another without change. The words with which we build our sermons will always mean whatever our hearers decide they mean. Careful craftsmanship can improve the likelihood that the hearers will settle on the same ideas which the speaker intended, but the sharing of meaning remains at best a precarious business.

An additional factor is that each of us carries a great deal of unfinished business around within ourselves. That which we have experienced before remains to help shape the way we react to that which we experience now. The response which a particular message elicits may have little to do with the message itself. The hearer who comes to church still angry over something that happened on the job may react to the sermon in surprising ways. Another person who had a bad experience with a former pastor may not listen at all.

This aspect of the communication process has such profound influence on the receiving of meaning that it may cause the complete reversal of messages. Robert Duke cites what he calls "the Mr. Bigot experiment." This was an experiment wherein "prejudiced people were fed anti-prejudiced propaganda. It was found that the people involved . . . actually used the data to reinforce their existing prejudices."[3]

On practical grounds alone it becomes clear that the people will help shape the preaching whether that participation is desired or not. There is no way to avoid it. Since the public proclamation of the gospel necessarily involves hearers as well as a speaker, a partnership exists that is fundamental to preaching. The sermon belongs to the church not only to possess, but to create.

Fortunately this is one of those happy situations in which it may be affirmed that what is, is that which ought to be. Theological considerations should cause us to seek partnership between pulpit and pew even if the practical necessities did allow a choice.

Sermons are possible in the first place because of the church. A sermon is not a valid event merely because the words spoken are correct and biblical. If so, it would be possible to preach to an empty room. Speaking only becomes a sermon when it takes place in relation to a congregation; preaching results when the church assembles together. It is not too much to say that the church creates that which, in turn, creates the church. Preaching has to do with the whole church rather than just an elite part of it.

Helmut Thielicke is one who holds that the church creates the sermon not only in grand theory but in practical reality.

> Time and again it has been my personal experience that hardly ever do we arrive at such vital, searching, and yet thematically broad discussions as when we talk over with others a text which is to be the basis of a sermon. Even common engagement in the task of interpretation is a stimulating thing, and the question of how the message is to be expressed leads us through far-flung and very exciting landscapes of human life.[4]

In saying this, Thielicke is not merely visualizing learned discussions among his fellow theologians. He has in mind something much more ordinary and available. Conversation with those who will eventually hear the sermon—the laity—adds a breadth of view which the professional person acting alone might not possess.

It is well to remember that Protestants have historically affirmed that the ministry of the church belongs to the whole people of God. The clergy function within the church, exercising gifts given by God so that others who have similarly received gifts may be helped to use them. In performing this necessary task, the preacher does not work in isolation. Gifts are shared with others who also have gifts to share. Preaching properly emerges from this give and take.

Therefore, for reasons practical and theological, it is appropriate to affirm that the sermon belongs to the church not only to possess, but to create. All of the people, clergy and laity alike, have responsibilities toward the preaching. It is a function of the whole church.

This view of preaching as an act which is appropriately shared with the whole congregation is the necessary starting point for preaching dialogically. It stands alongside another complimentary viewpoint which is also essential.

Dr. Carl R. Rogers has been a pioneer in emphasizing that each person possesses the capacities needed for growth and health. Rather than seeing his patients as needy persons who can only get well if he gives them something, Dr. Rogers has maintained that the patients already have what they need for health. His contribution is to provide the kind of relationship which will set them free to use what they already have.

> If I can provide a certain type of relationship, the other person will discover within himself the capacity to use that relationship for growth, and change and personal development will occur.[5]

The implications of that concept run in many directions. Those who have responsibility for facilitating the maturation of persons may find Rogers's thought speaking to them. It suggests that people of all ages do not so much need to be raised as to be assisted in raising themselves.

Rogers cites research indicating that children whose parents treat them with warm, egalitarian attitudes come sooner to emotional maturity, showing more originality and security than most other children. By the time they reach school age, such children are generally likeable, friendly leaders.

Between parents and children a substantial degree of dependency is appropriate to the relationship, but even here the attitude in which parents see children as potential equals, with great capacities for responsible action, is most growth-producing. Might it not be even more so in the pulpit-pew relationship where dependency is not a given?

We are dealing here with a certain way of looking at people. This perspective may be identified in this way with respect to the church: the congregation is a responsible body able to discern the will of God through the activity of the Holy Spirit. It does not need the preacher to say authoritatively what ought to be believed. The people are able to test thoughts and come to responsible Christian conclusions for themselves.

This way of looking at people who hear sermons is in radical opposition to the tendency to view the congregation as a collection of immature Christians who need to be straightened out. To be sure, some are immature and some do need straightening out, but *that is their responsibility*. The dialogical preacher understands that these people to whom he or she speaks are fully able to examine their own lives under the lordship of Jesus Christ, and to make the necessary adjustments and corrections. The preacher's function is to share gospel insights in such a way as to make available to the people a selection of truth from which each person, under the guidance of the Spirit of God, may draw that which will encourage his or her growth in the faith.

It is exactly this way of looking at people as persons who are no less responsible than the preacher which most effectively calls on the flock to make crucial decisions about their spiritual relationships.

> Permitting people to make their own decision is in a way the same as demanding that they make their own decision. If you let a child go in the store and give the child a quarter and say, "OK, you can spend this quarter," you've really put a burden on that child. Your temptation is to relieve that burden by picking out something. "Daddy, should I buy this?" "Well, it's your quarter." "Should I buy that?" "It's your quarter." Permitting that child a decision is demanding of that child a decision.[6]

Exactly the same thing can be done through inclusive preaching. It is possible to preach so that the listener is stimulated to do his or her own thinking and find a conclusion which belongs uniquely to that person. Permitting this to happen really demands that it happen. And when it happens, the decision that results has a force that would not be present if it were merely a matter of giving assent to the preacher's conclusion.

Historical Precedents

Such an approach to preaching might seem to be rather a new thing, but such is not the case. Current interest in this subject is only a revival of that which was inherent in preaching from the beginning, but which slipped from view along the way.

The roots of Christian preaching reach back to the Jewish synagogue. During a period of three centuries or so before the time of Christ there were great upheavals in the social and political world which challenged the traditional Jewish faith. Alexander the Great, and later the Roman conquest, forced Jews to take a stand on religious issues. There were also numbers of sects raising questions which required answers. Sermons became the primary means by which the rabbis provided the needed spiritual leadership.

According to Joseph Heinemann this was a creative time as the rabbis explored the possibilities of this new form of religious instruction. Preaching really produced a renewal of Judaism.

> The preacher succeeded in making the Bible an unceasing source of new meaning and inspiration. Through creative philology and

sometimes daring methods of interpretation, they overcame exegetical difficulties and imparted fresh significance to the Biblical stories and Biblical heroes, whom they transformed into ideal types. Shifts of emphasis took place, novel interpretations were offered of the Biblical text. The Bible itself, for example, was found to be the source of the Rabbi's own authority in the community, in place of the old leadership of the priests and prophets. . . .[7]

Preaching soon became an art form. In a day which offered little by way of amusement—at least by twentieth century standards—preaching was important for its entertainment value as well as its spiritual enrichment. Biblical stories were enlarged and ornamented. Storytelling and dramatization were used. Some preachers were highly theatrical, and were sometimes criticized for being more interested in entertainment than religious instruction. As a result, preachers who were widely known drew immense crowds.

Part of the appeal of Jewish preaching was its participatory nature. Religious exhortation was not thought to require a solemn, stately setting in order to be true to its purpose. The people joined in through variety of expressions, enjoying a level of freedom not typically associated with preaching as it is practiced today. Their laughter or rude comments showed whether the preacher's efforts were meeting approval or not. The speaker who did not capture the interest of the listeners was made quickly aware of that deplorable fact.

Questions from the congregations were an expected part of the preaching situation. The results could occasionally be embarrassing if the speaker had neglected preparation. Sometimes questions were raised which were beyond the ability of the preacher to answer, especially if he was inexperienced. That, however, was the exception rather than the rule. Preachers then as now usually understood the importance of preparation.

Compared with modern customs, there was much more freedom as to who might address the congregation. The synagogue service depended upon the participation of those present because there was no established leadership in the sense that there is today. The gathering of people for worship provided a forum for virtually anyone who wished to address the congregation. With the exception of the blessing, which was given by the priest if one was available, the entire service was in the hands of the worshippers. Anyone who wished to speak could do so, provided only that the head of the congregation granted permission. It was exactly this custom which made it possible for the Christian preachers to be widely heard in the synagogues. Today it is quite different; few contemporary churches would allow the apostle Paul to say a word!

So, from the beginning preaching was seen as part of a conversation carried on by the whole people of God. Laughter and tears, gaiety and solemnity ran together as the congregation shared life under the guidance of first one preacher and then another. If there was a question about a sermon, it was asked. If there was a comment prompted by the message, there was opportunity to give it. If one who had not spoken before had a message to contribute, he could be heard. Preaching was a community occasion.

Christian preaching naturally enough reflected the milieu out of which it sprang. Since Christianity was offered as the fulfillment of Judaism, and since its origins were totally within the Jewish community, it obviously started with Jewish forms.

In his book *Communicating the Gospel,* Dr. William Barclay focuses on a particular element which is important for understanding the earliest Christian preaching.

> The sermon was always followed by general discussion, and it was here that the Christian preacher got the greatest chance of all to communicate the Christian message. The word that we come on again and again in regard to the preaching of the Christians in the synagogue is the word *dispute* or *argue.* The Jews disputed with Stephen but could not meet his arguments (Acts 6:9-10). Paul argued in the synagogue at Thessalonica (Acts 17:2); he argued in the synagogue at Corinth (Acts 18:2); he argued in the synagogue at Ephesus (Acts 18:19). Here is the great basic fact of early preaching. *Early preaching was not a monologue but a dialogue.* It was not a question of one man telling a crowd of men; it was a case of a group of people talking it over together.[8]

Prior to Paul, of course, Jesus had followed the same pattern. The only glimpse we are given of his childhood shows us a twelve-year-old boy who has neglected his obvious obligations to his parents in order to ask questions of the teachers (Luke 2:41-51). At so early an age he was actively engaged in the "disputing" process so central to the practice of Judaism. The fact that even a youth could participate so freely with the religious scholars says much about the openness of the dialogue in which the community engaged.

Many of his teaching opportunities came as a result of informal questions put to him. He had access to the synagogues, including his own at Nazareth, though the outcome at Nazareth was unhappy (Luke 4:16-30). The violence of the reaction to his teaching at Nazareth may suggest something of the freedom and lack of inhibition inherent in preaching situations in those days. Today it is hardly expected that a sermon might be followed by open expressions of opposition, let alone by the formation of a lynch party!

The preaching of the early church which is recorded in the New Testament is unmistakably dialogical. Peter's sermon at Pentecost was a direct response to the question "What does this mean?" (Acts 2). His sermon in the temple grew directly out of the amazement of the crowd over the healing of the man lame since birth (Acts 3). Peter's preaching in the house of Cornelius answered the request which had come to him (Acts 10).

The dialogical pattern continued as the church moved outward into the Gentile world. One of the characteristics of Christian preaching was its flexibility; it began with whatever point of contact could be established with the available congregation and went on from there to tell of Jesus. Again Barclay has commented on Paul's practice in this connection.

> As a preacher Paul had an amazing gift for starting from where his audience was. His basic message is the same, but he had an astonishing gift of technique which enabled him to adapt that message to the audience which he was addressing.
>
> In Antioch of Pisidia he was addressing Jews in a Jewish synagogue. . . . When Paul spoke to this audience, he began in the Old Testament; he continued in the Old Testament; and he ended in the life of Jesus as fulfillment of the Old Testament. . . . In Athens, Paul's method was quite different. There he was not speaking in a Jewish synagogue but in the open air. He was not speaking to a Jewish audience, but to a Greek audience. He therefore began with quotations from the Greek poets and philosophers. . . . In Lystra once again Paul's method was quite different. In Lystra he was out in the wilds. . . . There Paul starts from the sun and the wind and the rain and from growing things—things which all men know.[9]

From the beginning preaching was thus seen as an activity involving the whole people; it was the business of all who were present. So it should continue to be. After all, everyone has a stake in the preaching; it is too important to be left just to the preachers. Preaching is a primary, basic way through which God approaches humankind. The words of Paul are eloquent: "It pleased God through the folly of what we preach to save those who believe" (1 Corinthians 1:21). Through preaching we may all be saved, the hearer by hearing and the preacher by preaching. It is a business in which all who will must be employed.

Nor is this a one-time-only matter. The need of preaching continues throughout the believer's lifetime, and must regularly engage the efforts of the Christian person. In the mystery of God's spiritual economy, that grace which is given once for all needs regular renewal to maintain the vitality of the link between God and the believer. The Christian life is better thought of as a pilgrimage than as a single event; in a pilgrimage there are many times when one needs to stop for a drink of water or a new set of directions for travel. So it is not one sermon in which we need to share, but many.

Perhaps as good a clue to the continuing need for preaching as any may be found in the comment of Clement Welsh: "At the time of the sermon a person is asked to do an astonishing thing: begin making ultimate sense of everything. Yet most of us have trouble making partial sense of even a few things."[10] There is a whole universe waiting to be grasped from a Christian perspective, and God's infinity beyond that. That will be more than enough to occupy a lifetime of energetic involvement in the preaching task which belongs to the whole church.

The Special Function of the Preacher

When it is said that preaching is the business of the whole church, there is no intention to imply that the congregation must be overtly involved in the preparation of the message. There will be times and places where such direct participation will be thought useful. Indeed, techniques which directly engage the people to help shape the message will be discussed in the next chapter. That, however, does not suggest that it must be done that way for preaching to be dialogical.

Those who are called to the ministry of preaching are called to exercise gifts given by God for the benefit of the people of God. The preacher does not have a ministry which may be identified apart from the ministry which is given to the whole church. The particular gifts given create for the preacher a special function within the congregation. It is the preaching task to create a sermon event which will encourage the people to sermonize within themselves. The preacher has the responsibility of stimulating the people to begin the creative task which belongs to the whole church.

Welsh expresses the broad view of the function which the preacher ought to perform: "The opportunity of the preacher . . . is to make the sermon that act of religious communication which enables the listener to begin to make religious sense of his universe."[11] Notice that it is not the sermon which is to make sense of the universe, but the listener. The sermon is to be the catalyst which causes the hearer to do that which he or she has had the capacity to do all along.

In the final analysis the sermon which occupies the church is far larger than the message delivered from the pulpit. The preacher's sermon is much more limited in scope; it has served its purpose when the many individuals present have been stimulated to think on their own, searching out divine truths and applications bearing on their own diverse situations. The sum total of all this creative work constitutes the sermon for the church that day. Since it has been created by the church, it belongs to it and affects it in ways that the preacher's sermon alone never can.

Depending upon one's point of view, this understanding of the special function of the preacher may be thought broader or narrower than a concept which would lead to monological preaching. The monological approach has at its root the assumption that it is the special task of the preacher to bring God's message for that moment to the people. To be the one who brings that message is no small honor and no small task. Indeed, the implications of such a responsibility are staggering.

It does seem more limited "merely" to take the responsibility for creating the kind of occasion in which people will be open to whatever specific and particular message God may have for them individually. But when one considers the diversity of needs which people have, as well as the fearful richness of the gifts which God has to give, accepting such a function is no small task. When one thinks of the difficulty with which the most spiritually sensitive among us sinners becomes open to God, it is clear that to attempt to preach in such a way as to open the door for direct encounter between man and God is an enormous task. It is much too large, in fact; God himself must make it possible if it is to happen at all. Standing before such a calling, one develops new appreciation for the ancient sailor's prayer, "O God, thy sea is so vast and my boat is so small."

The preaching tradition of black churches provides a convenient opportunity to see how the work of preaching may be done in such a way as to evoke answering sermons from the people. Probably the inner response is not all that different from what goes on in many white congregations on any Sunday, but the oral nature of black worship makes the process easier to examine.

In a black church there is an overriding sense that the sermon is something pastor and people do together. Preaching is a communal experience, a time in which pulpit and pew share the faith with one another. Such a partnership is possible because of the mutual commitment to be in holy conversation with one another. This kind of relationship cannot be generated by one side alone. It requires a preacher who sees it as appropriate that the people help preach the sermon; it equally calls for a congregation that considers that kind of response proper. Without such a combination the black style of worship could never have emerged. But of course this combination has been present in black worship from the beginning. A congregation that talks back to the preacher is a part of African culture.

To the observer who comes as an outsider, black preaching seems to rely overmuch on appeal to emotion. "Emotionalism" is a word which has been applied to the black worship style. Indeed, the degree of intimate personal involvement which occurs may be distressing and sometimes even offensive to those accustomed to a more controlled atmosphere for worship.

Those who speak from inside the black culture, however, assert that there is more here than may meet the eye of the casual witness. Emotion, yes. That is affirmed as a necessary part of worship. But not emotion alone. Professor Henry Mitchell has said it this way:

> Black worshippers want to be stirred; they want to have an emo-
> tional experience. But they also want to be stretched, or helped and
> fed. . . . When such content and imaginative delivery grips a con-
> gregation, the ensuing dialogue between preacher and people is the
> epitome of creative worship. Mass participation works to increase
> retention. The strength of the Black tradition at its best has the ability
> to combine fresh insight with impact—to feed the people and yet to
> shake them into a recognition that the Spirit of God is always moving,
> always dynamic.[12]

The free-flowing nature of many black sermons sometimes creates the impression that there is little behind them in the way of preparation. It is not hard to come to the assumption that anyone could easily enter into *that* kind of dialogue. But not so.

> The often unconscious assumption of Black preaching is that man
> brings to God his very best and asks him to take both preacher and
> congregation and make between them a sermon experience in which
> his word and will are proclaimed, with *power*.[13]

If one is committed to bring the "very best" that one possesses, then there must be a rigorous commitment to disciplined achieve-
ment. In the black tradition this is likely to be not so much evident in preparation for a specific sermon, which may indeed be largely

spontaneous, but in the careful mastering of the preaching craft as it relates to the people with whom the preaching will be shared. Just as the jazz musician is not free to elaborate on the theme until the musical craft has been mastered through hours of work, so the black preacher will not be able to lift up the people in worship until the necessary skills have been obtained through study and practice.

Any preacher in any tradition has essentially only words with which to work. Fortunately the words of the Christian faith constitute a vast wealth of resource, so that none may claim a lack of raw material. The church has a great store of symbols which speak to the human condition concerning the pains and joys of daily living. Using them makes it possible to evoke out of apparent loneliness the sense of being part of the great stream of Christian witnesses who walked the path ahead of us. One may also call forth strength and awaken principles which persons had not suspected they possess.

But to achieve those possibilities is a challenge. To take that great storehouse of potential found in any dictionary and use the words contained therein to help people experience the lively vitality of God's truth is a task of immense difficulty.

> [The preacher] must find ways to convey through the dynamics of his words and the interrelations of words the sensible reality embodied in such ancient "carriers of meaning" as God, Christ, Holy Spirit, reconciliation, redemption, salvation, sacrament, heaven, hell, faith, hope, love. In order to reach with words a people accustomed to communication through total sensory stimuli enwrapped in the convincing and attractive environments of electronic media, we must be able to unwrap and enwrap in similarly convincing and attractive ways the great words in which our Christian tradition is stored.[14]

To do that "unwrapping" and "enwrapping" in a way that invites the hearers' participation, in a way that entices the hearers to go beyond the preacher's insights to find their own truths, bearing on their own lives being lived before God, is an art and a calling worthy of any person. It is not clear whether there ever was a time when there was a secure place for the preacher who had not submitted to the discipline of the craft, but it is certainly clear that today is not that time.

The present need is for a weekly struggle with the Scriptures and with life, for a painful creativity that persists until an expression has been found which takes hold of both time and timelessness. We are followers of One who called his disciples to carry their own crosses. It should not be any surprise for the preacher to discover that the cross is real, it is painful, and it is often present in the preparation of sermons. Nor should anyone suppose that consistently helpful preaching can be managed apart from that necessary self-denial.

Dialogical preaching aims at a certain unfinished quality because there must be something left for the people to complete, some necessary work for them to do. Otherwise there can be no effective dialogue. The temptation may be to suppose that a sermon which wants less at the end can be safely launched with less at the beginning. This is definitely not so, for the dialogical preacher attempts a task even more difficult than that undertaken by the one who speaks monologically.

> How shall the preacher prepare himself for dialogical preaching?
> . . . he should study the theological resources of Scripture, history, and doctrine; and study *also,* with equal seriousness, what he knows of the related meanings from his own authority of both the traditional and contemporary experience; and how to recognize the authenticity of the dialogue, both historical and contemporary, between God and man and the dependence of each on the other. His purpose is to bring these dialogues together in order that the historical dialogue may be challenged and judged in the light of the contemporary; and the contemporary dialogue be challenged and given perspective by the historical.[15]

As described by Reuel Howe, that is a monumental undertaking. It is far more than any person working alone can hope to do. But the dialogical preacher knows not only that attempting such a task as a solitary individual is difficult, but also that it is unnecessary. The special function given the preacher is to set the process in motion. Once the sermonizing begins, the community will take it from there.

CHAPTER 4

Crafting the Dialogical Sermon

The decision to preach dialogically does not usher one into a new world filled with exotic techniques. Granted that a decision to develop the sermon from the base of a different intention may lead one to try methodologies not previously used, it remains true that the sermon forms of dialogic preaching have been with us for a long time. With the exception of certain multimedia possibilities recently made available by modern technology, there is nothing new under the sun in preaching. There may be a need to sharpen neglected skills, but one need not invent a replacement for the wheel. The radical differences are in the intent of the sermon and in the way the preacher and people perceive each other. Once those changes are accomplished, other concerns are quite manageable.

Probably too little attention is paid to the value which the relationship between pastor and people has for preaching. The fact that they recognize and trust each other is of great importance. Much of the strength of the message lies in the fact that it comes from one who knows those to whom the message is given. The word of a stranger may be a helpful change of pace, but people come week after week to hear their own pastor. For this reason, any preacher must know the people, but most especially is this true of the one who hopes to engage them in dialogue.

> When the pastor writes a sermon, an empathetic imagination sees again those concrete experiences with his people which called upon all his resources, drove him to the Bible and back again, and even now hang as vivid pictures in his mind. When a pastor preaches, he doesn't sell patent medicine; he writes prescriptions. Others may hurl epithets at the "wealthy" but the pastor knows a lonely and guilt-ridden man confused by the Bible's debate with itself over prosperity: Is prosperity a sign of God's favor or disfavor? Others may display knowledge of "poverty programs" but the pastor knows what a bitter thing it is to be somebody's Christmas project.[1]

As it happens, the ability to know people in this kind of way, which goes so far beyond surface appearance, is one of the primary qualities which Carl Rogers found in persons who are able to create and sustain helping relationships. Such people are able to share the intimate thoughts and feelings of another person by seeing them through the eyes of that other person. Such sensitivity allows the kind of mutual respect and acceptance which does not need either to agree or to judge.[2]

It is apparent that the preacher who seeks to create and maintain a helping relationship with the people by including them fully in preaching will begin by being a listener. There is no other way by which one may come to that degree of intimate knowlege about the persons with whom the sermon is to be shared. The actual preaching situation will be bracketed by listening before and after, searching not just for words but for understanding. By this kind of intense, deeply personal hearing the dialogical preacher not only obtains the insights into the congregation so essential to the sermon, but also begins the process of setting the people free to sermonize within themselves. There is something about being heard which enables people to hear.

An essay on interpersonal communication describes a carefully controlled set of experiments in which students were required to do a task at the instruction of their teacher. Some of the time they worked under conditions in which they could hear and be heard, that is, questions and answers could be exchanged between the instructor and the students. At other times the students could only listen and do the best they could with the instructions given. The combined series of experiments demonstrated that accuracy is in direct relationship to the opportunity for feedback.[3]

Perhaps most important was the discovery that a class working under conditions which permitted a free exchange of questions and answers performed rationally and logically, unless class members recently had been working under conditions in which they could not respond to the instructions given. In that case, much hostility was expressed. The conclusion was that the inability to give feedback creates hostility even when simple matters are concerned. There is something about not being heard which produces within people conditions which make it hard for them to hear!

Interestingly enough the same experiment disclosed that when instructors were restricted to one-way communication with their students, although the students had a low degree of confidence in the situation, the instructors had even less confidence. In a no-feedback situation the students could at least compare their work with the instructions given, while the instructors had no way of knowing how the students were feeling. The circumstances which produced hostility in the students produced feelings of uncertainty and inadequacy in the teachers. It is not only the congregations which benefit from the listening inherent in dialogical preaching. The preacher actually may have more to gain.

What is being discussed is a way of living with people so that they are constantly included. The thoughts, questions, hopes, fears, beliefs, and doubts of the people to whom the sermon will eventually come are not at all extraneous to the sermon. These are the very matters which the message is intended to address most urgently. They need to be included at the beginning.

Listening to the Congregation

Dialogical preaching, then, begins and ends with listening. The sermon becomes part of a continuing conversation which started well before the preacher went to the pulpit, and which continues after the benediction. The pattern of listening for meanings beneath the spoken words is built into the relationship which binds congregation and pastor together.

Sometimes it may be thought desirable to formalize the listening through the use of planned occasions devoted to that purpose. In general there are three main approaches which can be used for this, though of course there are endless variations.

A Sermon Seminar

One model which has been widely suggested is the sermon seminar. The preacher meets with a group which comes together specifically to help launch the preparation for a sermon that will be delivered a week or two later. Typically the minister will start the session with a brief introduction to the sermon text, providing a short exegesis to aid in initial understanding. Some passages lend themselves to more dramatic approaches. Parables, for instance, may be acted out in role plays. Such an involvement is not only enjoyable, but also it frequently produces unexpected insights as biblical characters literally come alive for the group.

Whatever the means used to open up the text, a period of discussion follows. This is the preacher's chance to ask questions, to raise issues, and to press for clarification. The temptation for the minister to become the teacher at this time needs to be resisted. Now is the time for the group to help the preacher; allowing that role to be reversed will stifle the creativity of the occasion and defeat its purpose.

During the period of discussion the pastor will be making notes, at least mentally. It will become clear that certain information needs to be provided in the sermon to aid understanding, and certain questions need to be addressed. It will be equally clear that other matters which the sermon might well have fastened on are of little interest or concern to the laity, and these can be avoided. Sometimes the minister discovers that she or he does not personally understand the text as well as had been supposed, so additional study will be required. Frequently insights will be generated which could not be found in any commentary.

Sermon seminars do not replace any preparation which would otherwise have occurred. Rather, they add an additional helpful step. They also do not shift the responsibility for content or interest of the finished product. The seminar group properly recognizes that the preacher retains full responsibility for whatever appears in the message that is ultimately delivered. The preacher understands that the lay colleagues are not to be blamed if it turns out to be one of those days when the sermon oozes out over the congregation and settles like a gelatinous mass.

Unquestionably the sermon developed in such a shared way will be different from one which did not have the benefit of that collaboration. Two of the sermons presented in chapter 5 had this kind of assistance.

Major days in the Christian year have always been difficult preaching times for the writer. On such days one dare not get far from the story being celebrated. Indeed, one would never want to do that. But so *much* has already been said. How may the story be retold with fresh vitality?

One year the approach of Easter was especially frustrating. In spite of considerable prayer, meditation, and study, no compelling idea was forthcoming for the Easter sermon. The dilemma was frankly shared with a men's prayer group, who volunteered to come together for a sermon seminar. The result was the inspiration which led to "The Man God Wouldn't Forget" (see chapter 5).

Two crucial insights were generated within the group which jointly provided the framework for this message. One was the oddity of Peter being singled out from the rest of the disciples. The other was the probability that the resurrection of Jesus was terrifying to one who had denied him after promises of faithfulness were so earnestly made. This latter thought seems so self-evident that one feels it ought always to have been known; yet the writer had never thought of it and possesses no commentary which contains that suggestion.

"A Word for Losers" (see chapter 5) was also shared with lay friends in its development. This sermon came in the middle of a series about characters in the Gospels. One of the aims of the series was to help the people recognize the biblical persons as flesh and blood humans like themselves, so that a sense of relationship to their own lives could be established.

The seminar group role-played the text, and then got caught up in an imaginative description of the woman and the husband whom she had betrayed (p. 118). During the ensuing discussion someone asked, "Where was her lover?" (p. 116). Another asked, "Why did they leave in order of their age?" (p. 116). Ultimately the group came to its own conclusion that it is not the strong and the proud but rather the weak and the humble who have a place before God (pp. 120-123).

"A Word for Losers" probably has more material directly derived from the seminar group than would typically be the case, but a sermon now and then in which people can recognize a good bit of their own insight is healthy. One aspect of the greatness of Dr. Martin Luther King, Jr., as a preacher was his extraordinary ability to articulate truths which the people themselves carried in the deep places of their own lives, but which they did not know how to speak. Frequently Dr. King was not persuading at all, but rather expressing what the people already knew in their bones must be so. Giving voice to the convictions of the congregation is an honorable, useful, and helpful function for the sermon.

A cautionary word is also in order concerning the sermon seminar method of listening. Although many writers advocate it enthusiastically, little substantial research is available to document its value. The writer undertook such research to test the assumption that this approach would enhance sermon effectiveness, not only for those who took part, but also for all hearers. "Sermon effectiveness" was identified in terms of the likelihood that preaching would produce life-change in its hearers. An effective sermon would be expected to produce inner spiritual or emotional changes and/or outward behavioral changes among those who heard it, those changes being consistent with the goals and gospel understandings of the preacher.

Pastors and laity from eleven congregations representing a variety of Protestant denominations were involved in the study.

A total of 428 responses was received, some from persons who had participated in seminar groups and others from persons who had not. Some unfortunate weaknesses in the survey form clouded the results, but it is sufficiently clear that the sermons delivered by the eleven preachers who shared in this project did not fulfill the expectations one might logically have had for messages prepared with the benefit of lay insight.

A major reason is that effective use of sermon preparation groups apparently requires unexpected skill on the part of the preacher. Incorporating useful suggestions of the small group into the living fabric of the sermon eventually delivered is a more subtly difficult task than would appear on the surface. Those who choose to work with this methodology should recognize the need to develop a mature skill before making assumptions that it is producing the sermonic benefit ultimately available. This is, after all, an approach to sermonizing for which few have been trained.

Having recognized that the seminar is not a magic cure-all automatically guaranteeing better preaching, the fact remains that it is a most useful way to sharpen one's listening skills. For at least two decades preachers have found that the occasional use of this approach has had a stimulating, helpful effect. Many who have not yet made use of it will surely want to acquaint themselves with its possibilities.

Post-Sermon Feedback

Other ways of formalizing the listening process focus on obtaining feedback after the sermon rather than input beforehand. The talk-back session is used in some congregations. The minister establishes an open forum, either in the sanctuary or in another room following the benediction. The people are invited to ask questions or make comments. During this time the congregation can ask questions for clarification and express support or disagreement as people choose. Responses can be made not just to the preacher, but also to each other; in this way individuals can contribute to the sermon. There are opportunities for misunderstandings to be clarified.

The usefulness of the talk-back session hinges largely upon the willingness of the congregation as a whole, or at least in significant part, to participate in this kind of activity. Churches differ widely at this point. Some congregations enter into the forum experience with enthusiasm, while other congregations are not interested. It is important that the preacher not impose personal needs for dialogue on the congregation; to do so would be to act monologically, because in this instance the needs and concerns of the congregation would not be included in the decision to press for the forum experience.

Another way to obtain feedback involves a much smaller group, so that this method can be used in most congregations. Six to ten people are invited to meet following the service to provide the preacher with reaction to the sermon. This "feedback team" does not need to have leadership appointed in advance, although that is an option. Usually a set of questions will be provided in order to give some sense of structure, and in order to make sure the group addresses the concerns of the pastor. This is appropriate because in this style the feedback is being given specifically for the benefit of the preacher by persons who have volunteered to render such service. It is usually most productive for the preacher to be absent. A tape recorder is used to preserve the comments, and the preacher will listen to the tape at a later time.

This method offers benefits both to the lay participants and to the minister. Feedback team members end up with a sense of participating in the pulpit ministry of the church which they would be unlikely to obtain any other way. They also become caught up in the struggle to understand gospel meanings, with the result that they may experience the Word with that clarity and power which seem to come to those who have deep personal involvement.

For their part, preachers have few opportunities which can so quickly help them learn their strengths and weaknesses in oral communication. It also is an exceptionally helpful way to learn more about the people themselves. The thought processes of at least some of the congregation are laid bare as they invest themselves in the work of the feedback team. The reflective preacher will find this invaluable for planning future sermons.

None of the foregoing is intended to suggest that the listening stance so critical to dialogical preaching requires the use of formalized structures to obtain insights and reactions from the people. Most churches have a variety of small groups meeting for other purposes. Any Bible study, discussion, or prayer group provides at least indirect dialogue with the preaching ministry. All of these can readily be used to support the preacher's necessary intake of information, as Clyde Reid has documented.[4]

It may also be noted that valuable dialogue can and does take place in the absence of any formal group setting. The preacher who makes it a point to be with people individually as much as possible, and is open and nondefensive in attitude, will find the people raising questions and making comments pro and con about something said from the pulpit. The one who begins preparation for preaching by honing the listening skills will hear much that is enriching for the sermon that is yet to be.

Of course there is also the risk—virtually the certainty—that the skillful listener will sometimes hear things painful to receive. While not all such painful comment will be valid, this is the very material to which the preacher most urgently needs access if pulpit skills are to be brought to maturity. The temptation which this writer has is to respond with a defensive comment to explain away the criticism. Such a reaction does not encourage the trust which would allow future open sharing. When negative feedback is being given, it may be helpful to bear in mind that the times for speaking and the times for listening are often separate, distinct occasions. The listening times ordinarily do not require any response at all except for a word of appreciation for the sharing and a promise to think further about what has been said.

Listening in the Study

In dialogical preaching the same listening attitude carries over into the study where the formal preparation begins with the exposition of the Scriptures. In this connection it might seem fair to assume that all preaching begins with the preacher "listening" to the Scriptures. But it is quite possible to prepare a sermon with only a passing glance at the Bible; the writer has done so often enough! Beyond that—and much more damaging—it is possible to spend extended time handling the Scriptures without really allowing them the opportunity to speak for themselves. The assumptions which the reader brings to the text may effectively block out the message. The sermon which is prepared with little reference to the Bible has at least the merit that its condition is readily apparent to the congregation. It is much harder for the hearer to call to account the message which has incorporated many biblical words, while failing to grasp the substance of those words.

This is a concern which has been addressed by James D. Smart in his book *The Old Testament in Dialogue with Modern Man*. The explanation for the book includes this comment.

> When one hunts through volumes of American sermons for instances of preaching on Old Testament texts, one becomes aware that an acute situation in this area exists. . . . More than one volume of sermons that have been heralded as a brave attempt to let the Old

Testament speak have proved, on close examination, to reveal very little of the Biblical author's mind and a much larger measure of the preacher's mind on subjects only remotely connected with the Scripture under consideration.[5]

It is possible to pack a sermon full of biblical quotations and references without ever taking the Scriptures seriously. Indeed, those who have the most Bible in their sermons may be preaching it the least, using it instead merely to illustrate and support their own thoughts and categories. Such ideas as the preacher may generate may be wise and thoughtful, but that is hardly the same as proclaiming the Word of God. It is far better preaching to take a single passage and concentrate on drawing out the meanings which are inherent in that bit of Scripture.

In the study the dialogical preacher has an advantage which others may lack. Having learned to be comfortable—or at least capable—in listening to fellow Christians without having always to answer back, it may possibly be more tolerable to listen to the Word of God without having to insist that it say what we have always supposed it means.

Whether that is true or not, the preacher who seriously intends to facilitate the divine conversation between God and the people will use all of the exegetical tools available to be sure that the Word of God has been truly heard. Such listening to the Scriptures will usually precede the selection of a sermon theme or the development of a statement of purpose. Where circumstances dictate that the message for a particular time must be geared to a specific theme or purpose, extra attention should be given to make sure that the proposed development proceeds organically from the supporting text, so that homiletical rape is not committed in an effort to appear timely. To do otherwise is to deal monologically with the Scriptures. One is not likely to preach dialogically from such a beginning.

Selecting Sermon Forms

The most public evidence of a decision to preach in a manner that includes the listeners fully is the form selected for the sermon. And that requires a bit of explanation.

Halford Luccock once made this observation about form in preaching.

> In the craftsmanship of the preacher first place must be given to one of the basic principles of much modern architecture, "form follows function." That applies all the way from a chair to a skyscraper. If it is a chair, why not make something to sit on, instead of a disguised featherbed? If a gymnasium is being built, why make a Gothic ca-

thedral? The previous question is always, "What is the function of this talking?"[6]

We have previously seen that the function of preaching is more than the conveyance of information. Preaching aspires to create a moment of revelation, a salvation moment in which the shoes instinctively come off because there is the certain knowledge that one has unexpectedly come upon holy ground; God and person are face-to-face. That dialogical function calls for forms appropriate to the task.

The writer has a vivid memory of attending a Thanksgiving service. The preacher selected as his text one of Paul's bursts of praise which punctuate at random the letter to the Romans. None of the lively, irrelevant, joyful enthusiasm of the original comment was allowed to seep into the message. What was originally a spontaneous exclamation of the unutterable joy of being in Christ was reduced to a series of scholarly propositions. One by one they marched in neat, orderly, and rather gloomy procession until the sermon had run its course. The preacher's expression was consistently solemn as he spoke of joy; his tones were at times funereal as he urged the people to be thankful in their hearts. A dried prune is not more lacking in vital juices than the treatment accorded that text! A week later someone commented, "That sermon ruined my Thanksgiving. I just felt sad the whole day."

Preaching needs to be in forms which encourage an experience similar to that created by the original expression of the Word. The Thanksgiving preacher, having selected a text which was essentially a doxology, would have done better to have highlighted Paul's mood when those exclamations of praise were inserted into what is otherwise an orderly presentation, and then led the people in singing the doxology. That way they might well have had an experience comparable to the joy felt by those Christians in Rome who first received the letter.

Is the text the story of Adam and Eve, or perhaps of Gideon or Samson? The dialogical preacher will not merely offer a series of propositions about the story; rather the story will be told—told in modern idiom and setting perhaps, but unmistakably told. Is it a parable today? Then let a parable be put forth, possibly one which reverses the meaning of the familiar biblical parable which contains the message for the day. Through such a device the people will experience something of the shock elicited when Jesus told stories which ran counter to the familiar teachings of the day and so be sensitized to hear the biblical parable as though for the first time.

Or does one dare to speak of the incredible drama of crucifixion and resurrection? The pulpit should recreate the pain, the fear, and the ecstasy of that story which has surpassing power to save.

The writer has been captured by the story of the transfiguration. Realization came one day that what was obviously a crucial experience for Jesus and those privileged to be witnesses had never been adequately understood by this later witness. Resolve grew to make it one's own, and then to share that with the congregation. Far more than customary study went into the initial preparation. At the end there was a sense of being overwhelmed by the grace of God revealed in that extraordinary event.

An immediate problem developed when the time came to write the actual sermon. The amount of background material to be conveyed as an aid to understanding was enormous. The first outline was well suited for an academic lecture, but poor stuff for a sermon. The great danger was that the people would end up well informed about the transfiguration without ever experiencing it. Worst of all, they could even be bored. How sad to know the objective facts but be untouched by the electric power of this act of God! How could the message which might produce such an outcome be called biblical preaching?

It was decided to begin again, using the form of an eyewitness account. This would allow a great quantity of explanatory detail to be woven directly into the narrative without it appearing as a series of distracting sidelights. It would also help focus more sharply that material which was truly critical to understanding, making it easier to omit other interesting but less vital data. Such an approach also opens the door to increased use of nonverbal communication— dramatic forms permit information to be conveyed through a single gesture which would otherwise take a paragraph of text.

Most important, the sense of personal involvement is intrinsic to an eyewitness account. Few experiences in life are so involving as hearing another tell of a great event in which that person has been caught up. The result of this approach was "Speechless" (see chapter 5).

This sermon is really pictorial preaching, as is all storytelling. Word pictures communicate with a closeness and clarity rarely to be achieved through proposition and logic. Intellectual sophisticate and functional illiterate are both glad when truth comes wrapped in the warmth of a story. Illustrations are not merely windows letting in light to illumine the message; rather the message is in the illustration.

It was not by accident that Jesus used parables at crucial moments. Nor is it accidental that so much of Scripture consists of the telling of stories, showing us living people in common situations illustrating eternal truths. This kind of language takes hold of the whole person, including but not limited to the logical, reasoning mind.

Considerations of form extend also to the basic organization of the sermon. Essentially there are two choices available: a message may be organized deductively or inductively.

Deductive Sermons

The deductive sermon is neat, orderly, and logical. Near the beginning the central theme or key idea is announced. This is the main point which the preacher wishes the hearers to accept. That theme will be elaborated and supported by a series of subpoints which follow in turn. Three subpoints supporting the main theme form a common pattern, though more or less may be used. Each of the propositions offered as a subpoint will be explained and illustrated so that the hearer will be able to understand the speaker's meaning. At the end the presentation will be summarized briefly so that the message stands as a unit complete in itself.

Deductive organization has been an effective sermon form for centuries. Its clarity appeals to the orderly mind. Since all of the energy is focused on driving home a single key thought, that purpose can be well accomplished. In the hands of a skillful preacher the deductive sermon is a powerful tool.

It is not, however, dialogical. Since it concentrates on conveying and selling the preacher's idea, it is not well suited for encouraging the hearer to value her or his own thoughts. Since it begins by announcing the conclusion, there is little likelihood of an element of surprise remaining for the end. The hearer is almost encouraged to tune out since it is already known where the sermon is going. The congregation is not encouraged to meet the Scriptures with their original impact because the propositions developed by the preacher are the most important parts of the sermon. The tendency is for the Scriptures to support the preacher rather than the other way around.

Perhaps the most difficult aspect of deductive preaching for today's hearer is that no insight is given as to the means by which the conclusion was reached. The proposition with which the sermon begins is a conclusion settled upon in the study; supporting it with other propositions is not at all the same as sharing the process by which the conclusion was developed originally. Since today's hearers have been trained from childhood to look not only at answers, but also to ask how those answers were reached, it is quite possible for the deductive sermon to lose its hearers with the first sentence. Even if they agree to come along, they do so under conditions which do not evoke their ability to do independent thinking.

Inductive Sermons

An alternative form which is more congenial to the dialogical purpose is the inductive sermon. In this style a series of particular points or illustrations is given, with the general conclusion being drawn only at the end. The speaker immediately has gained the advantage of listener interest. Individual details are shared one at a time, but there is no hint where the sermon is going until it gets there. The hearer becomes engaged in trying to fit the pieces together to find the unifying theme, but still the element of surprise is there for the ending.

No doubt part of the ability of inductive preaching to maintain listener interest is also due to the fact that it is a form which is more related to life, and therefore seems more pertinent. After all, life is lived inductively rather than deductively. No parent struggles with childhood, but only with specific children. The electrician may be completely unable to speak of the universal properties of electricity, but the house gets wired anyway. At the laundry there is little concern for the chemical reactions involved when clothing is immersed in a solution containing a cleansing agent, but the detergent is still carefully measured. The preacher discusses the universal mortality of all flesh and meets only apathy in response. When it is announced that Mr. Johnson has terminal cancer, the church comes alive.

This is exactly the style of the Bible. Rather than discussing the origins of humanity in general terms, it tells of a specific couple. Jesus did not rely on abstractions to explain the kingdom of God; rather he said, "There was a woman who lost a coin. . . ." Paul did not write to Philemon to discuss general problems of slavery. The burden of the letter was, "Now let us talk about Onesimus."

Since the Bible is largely inductive, this form is particularly well suited for letting the Bible speak for itself. The Bible stories can be told and experienced, with conclusions drawn at the end of the experience. Indeed, it may be that the preacher will not offer any conclusions at all. Jesus often left it to the hearer to figure out what the parables meant; we might today dare to do the same thing. Inductive preaching invites the congregation to provide the conclusion—not orally and corporately, but individually and inwardly. Since something essential is left for the hearer to do, it is clear to all that the congregation's participation is valued and needed.

"Two Foolish People" (see chapter 5) is an example of a sermon deliberately left incomplete. Structurally the sermon could hardly be simpler. It consists essentially of four stories. By far the bulk of attention is given to the middle two, which together retell the biblical account of Elijah and the widow of Zarephath. The closing story is very brief, sketching in just enough detail to place the life of Christ in juxtaposition to Elijah and the widow. There are no connecting links provided to tie the several stories together, except that each story has internal similarities in its ending. There is no hint of a conclusion. Questions are sprinkled throughout, but few answers are given. At the end the sermon simply stops, swiftly and unexpectedly. It has little meaning except as the listener contributes meaning to it.

Learning to live with incompleteness so that the congregation could have room for its contribution was the most difficult aspect of the writer's personal experience when he began to preach inductively. All of the prior homiletical training and experience had been reinforcing the view that it is the preacher's task to tell the people what the Scriptures mean. When the time came that it was no longer possible to accept that view of preaching, there were several months in which every sermon was accompanied by guilt feelings because it did not seem that the whole job had been done. Even though those feelings were judged to be inappropriate, they were real and had strong impact.

Yet it was undeniable that the people for whom those sermons were prepared were intelligent men and women who were capable of all sorts of decisions about other aspects of their lives. If they could be encouraged to see themselves as capable of finding their own applications of the Christian faith, they would be far better equipped to practice that faith in all of their dealings on a day-to-day basis. It was a matter of encouraging them to draw upon the spiritual resources which they already possessed.

After all, most people who hear a sermon have already heard many other sermons. They have had religious instruction. They have been part of spiritual conversations. Even if a rare person should be found who has had none of those, everyone still has lived. People do not come empty to church. One of the tasks of preaching is to help people use that which they already possess, stimulating them to call up and apply relevant insights out of that vast amount which every person has in storage.

One of the premier examples of the power of an inductive sermon to evoke from its hearers the resources needed to complete the message is the sermon which A. J. Gossip preached immediately after the death of his wife, "But When Life Tumbles In, What Then?" It is a network of Scripture, personal comments, and illustrations from the arts which are woven together to make a single fabric, but in such a way that the pattern is only visible from the end looking back. The listener or reader who progresses through the sermon has no idea where it is leading, but is so completely captured by it that it is nearly impossible to put it aside.

> The first, and possibly the most overwhelming, impression which the sermon makes is its intensely personal nature. The preacher gives the impression of conversing with a close, even an intimate friend, as he talks quietly about the great loss he has suffered. Even the biblical material and profound eloquence of Gossip's sermon become secondary in the setting of that confidential revelation of human feelings. It would be as impossibly rude not to listen to this sermon as to ignore a friend who looks us in the eyes and tells us about the loss of his wife.[7]

For instance, who could hear such a statement as this from one sharing his own grief and fail to relate it to experiences within their own lives?

> I do not understand this life of ours. But still less can I comprehend how people in trouble and loss and bereavement can fling away peevishly from the Christian faith. In God's name, fling to what? Have we not lost enough without losing that too? If Christ is right—if, as He says, there are somehow, hidden away from our eyes as yet, still there, wisdom and planning and kindness and love in these dark dispensations—then we can see them through. But if Christ was wrong, and all that is not so; if God set His foot on my home crudely, heedlessly, blunderingly, blindly, as I unawares might tread upon some insect in my path, have I not the right to be angry and sore? If Christ was right, and immortality and the dear hopes of which He speaks do really lie a little way ahead, we can manage to make our way to them. But if it is not so, if it is all over, if there is nothing more, how dark the darkness grows! You people in the sunshine may believe the faith, but we in the shadow must believe it. We have nothing else.[8]

The arts are in this sermon: Goethe and Dante and a picture from the National Gallery of Art. The Scriptures are there too—

Jeremiah, Ezekiel, the psalmist, and most of all Christ. And the humanity of the preacher is openly shared, not in the abstract and general, but in the painfully specific: "There is one thing I should like to say which I have never dared to say before, not feeling that I had the right."[9]

At the end there is an ending. It is not a conclusion at all. A conclusion would be impossible, for there is so much left for the congregation to complete. Rather there is simply a statement of the preacher's own faith, brought forth to share with the people in a time of great personal loss.

> I don't think you need be afraid of life. Our hearts are very frail; and there are places where the road is very steep and very lonely. But we have a wonderful God. And as Paul puts it, what can separate us from His love? Not death, he says immediately, pushing that aside at once as the most obvious of all impossibilities.
>
> No, not death. For, standing in the roaring of the Jordan, cold to the heart with its dreadful chill, and very conscious of the terror of its rushing, I too, like Hopeful, can call back to you who one day in your turn will have to cross it, "Be of good cheer, my brother, for I feel the bottom, and it is sound."[10]

As one would expect with any form which lends itself to the creative imagination, the inductive method can be developed in a variety of ways. One of these ways is termed "the problem solution." This type of development divides itself into two sections. The first section introduces a problem, establishing its own particular relevance for that audience and lifting up the various aspects which contribute to its complexity. The remaining section helps people understand where the solution lies, particularly helping them see how the gospel bears on this problem.[11]

Perhaps the largest hazard with this particular variety of inductive preaching is the temptation to overdevelop the problems at the expense of the solution. It is, after all, relatively much easier to describe the difficulty than to marshal the resources which will overcome the difficulty. But with due consideration given to keeping an adequate balance, that concern disappears.

Another way to develop the inductive form is extremely simple for the preacher, and yet it is particularly appreciated by those who listen to the message because of its ability both to hold their interest and to engage the use of their minds. In this style one simply retraces in the pulpit the steps which were previously taken in the study.

Remember that preparatory work is always inductive. One takes a passage and jots down random ideas which spring from it.

The text is examined bit by bit as one layer of meaning after another is explored. Commentaries will be consulted. Perhaps there are clippings in the file which are called forth by the text. As the specific bits of information accumulate, one begins to formulate some thought which captures the essence of the biblical message. Perhaps there will be several trials, and none is quite right. Eventually there is an idea which seems to contain all that is important for this time and this place. One has a sense of having captured it at last—or, more accurately, of having been captured by this grand idea which has been there in Scripture all along, but which has just now been revealed in a fresh way to the searching preacher. It is a rich moment, a powerful moment. Revelation has occurred. It is a time of salvation.

If a deductive form is to be used for the sermon, the message will begin at this point. The gripping discovery which came as the conclusion to patient inductive work in the study will become the thesis with which the deductive sermon begins. Whether that key idea is actually stated or not, it will control the entire sermon as the various points are developed to support it in the hope that the hearers will be persuaded to adopt this idea as their own.

But suppose that the preacher might simply share the journey which was traveled in reaching that exciting moment of discovery. What might happen then? One can become a reporter of a specific search which that specific person has undertaken. "I knew this passage so well that I began with a certain assumption. . . . But as I looked at it again a question began to nag. . . . In trying to answer the question, I discovered something from history which I had never known. . . . That took me off on a side trip as I became interested in a different aspect. . . . Suddenly my breath was taken away as God gave me a thought which I had never had before. . . ." Such a walk down the path of discovery under the guidance of one who has been there before often allows the hearer to make the same discovery. And because, under those circumstances, it is truly the hearer's discovery, this new truth has an excitement and an ownership not likely to be produced through other means.

Among the sermons included in chapter 5, the one which best exemplifies this variation of inductive preaching is "A Word for Losers." Of course one does not burden the congregation with every technical detail uncovered in the commentaries, but the major steps taken during a rather frustrating time of preparation are there. The people are made aware that textual problems exist. Questions which could not be adequately answered are indicated, and time

shared with a sermon seminar group is mentioned. A pair of observations about the text is included, and an illustrative side trip
is taken together. All of this leads ultimately to a pair of truths,
one or the other of which should be a point of identification for
every person who might hear this message.

With this particular approach to inductive preaching, there are
two temptations which one must guard against. One temptation
is to be unrealistically modest and assume that the congregation
will not be interested in so intimate an account of this bit of one's
own personal history. "Surely the people would rather have great
ideas and would be bored by the details of my study!" In practice
the opposite is true. Nothing is more interesting than to be permitted to look over the shoulder of a particular person who is
finding the way to a truth which one instinctively knows will
involve one. Knowing that there is likely to be a great idea waiting
at the end of the search simply adds to the suspense.

The other temptation develops with growing familiarity with
this particular style. Since the sermon consists of the sharing of a
series of random experiences, and since it is at its best when it is
open-ended and incomplete, it becomes easy to assume that the
message can be prepared with a minimum of effort. It would seem
that the sharing of any set of experiences will do. And if one is
given permission to talk about oneself anyway, there are all sorts
of stories which can be told.

But of course not just any set of experiences will bring the
people the excitement of discovery; nor will they have the same
interest in every detail of the preacher's life as they will have toward
those moments in which the Scriptures are being earnestly searched
on their behalf.

The fact is that rigid discipline is as necessary to the helpful
use of this method as it is to any other form of preaching. If the
study has not been pursued until a moment of genuine discovery
has been reached, there is not likely to be much waiting for the
congregation when all make the trip together. And if the elements
of study which are to be reported are not carefully selected for their
ability to help move the people along, then they may not be brought
along at all, but may simply be left bored and bewildered.

An additional word should be said about closure with respect
to preaching in a dialogical way which includes the insights and
concerns of the hearers. Within the evangelical tradition it is common, perhaps even normative, for the message to end with a call
to commitment, an invitation to act in faith in response to the call

of Christ extended to every person to come and follow. There is no conflict between the need for dialogical preaching to be open-ended and the need for an appropriate opportunity for the hearers to express their commitment in response to the message which has been shared.

All that is needed is the recognition that the sermon and the response to the sermon are separate events. One may follow the other with but a few seconds of silence between. The people will recognize and appreciate the difference between the two elements of the worship experience. Since the people are now being asked to respond to a message with insights which are most truly their own, there will be added impact to the invitation.

The strongest invitation, however, seems to be the one which is separated from the sermon by a significant interval. At the end of the sermon the preacher may sit down and allow some moments for reflective silence before proceeding. Or a musical selection may follow the sermon with great effectiveness, especially if it is well chosen to support the emphasis of the message. Any approach which provides some *reflective* time before the invitation makes it more likely that there will be faith decisions wanting to be expressed.

Through dialogical preaching the sermon can become a shared event in which both the preacher and the people bring their meanings to contribute to the preaching. In such an inclusive setting preaching becomes a ministry of the whole church. The most critical factor in letting this happen is the initial perception that preaching does belong to the whole congregation, not only to possess, but to create. Once that perception has been obtained, the actual techniques are mostly familiar and comfortable, though perhaps underused—storytelling, parables, drama, and inductive organization are all effective in including the people in the preaching.

CHAPTER 5

Four Sermons

The following sermons are samples of the dialogical style. Some were prompted by the need to speak to special days within the calendar, such as Easter. Others grew from texts which seemed to need expression shared with the people of God at worship. Two had direct participation from lay people in their preparation. All were affected by the questions and comments of the people for whom they were prepared.

The Man God Wouldn't Forget (Mark 16:1-8)

"But go, tell his disciples and Peter that he is going before you to Galilee. . . ."

There's something strange in that text. The whole Easter story as Mark tells it fits together in natural sequence, except for one detail. The women who came early in the morning found that the grave carved out of rock in the hillside had been opened. The dead body they expected to find wasn't there. Instead there was a young man wearing a robe of unnatural brightness. We understand that he was an angel, a messenger of God. Messengers always have a message to deliver, and this one is no exception:

You seek Jesus of Nazareth, who was crucified. He has risen, he is not here; see the place where they laid him. But go, tell his disciples and Peter that he is going before you to Galilee; there you will see him, as he told you.

"Tell his disciples and Peter. . . ." That's what puzzles me. Why is Peter singled out? Why should any of them be singled out? But if one is singled out, why should it be Peter? It's as though God were saying, "Tell Peter I wouldn't forget him." If such a message is given, why not to John, to whom Jesus was apparently closest to all?

75

Let's go back a couple of days, to the Friday before. Jesus had been subjected to the form of execution reserved for the worst enemies of the state. Spikes were pounded through his hands and feet to impale him to timbers joined together in the shape of a cross. The purpose wasn't to kill him directly, but rather to place him in agony for the six to seven days it would take a man to die of exposure. He fooled them, however, and died in the short time of only six hours.

Then they had a problem. It was midafternoon when Jesus died. The sabbath would begin at sundown, and this particular sabbath was a high holy day. On that day bodies could not remain on crosses, nor could they be buried. The solution was a hasty burial carried out before sundown. A rich man made his own tomb available and Jesus' body was put in it. The body was quickly wrapped in the linen winding strips that were used for burials, but there wasn't time for the usual cleansing and anointing with spices. The sabbath, which prohibited work, ended at sundown Saturday, but nothing could be done in the dark. It would have to wait until there was light on Sunday.

Very early on Sunday three women who had been close to Jesus made their way to the tomb. They timed their arrival so that they'd be there at the moment it first became light. Their purpose was to anoint the body with burial spices so that it might be said that everything possible had been done for this man whom they loved.

How do you suppose the women expected to get into the tomb? It was closed with a heavy stone, a seal had been placed on it to make sure it stayed closed, and a guard of soldiers was there to enforce its security. How could they expect to get in?

There's a writing from the period, called *The Gospel of Peter,* which suggests that they may not really have expected to have access to the body. This is part of what it says:

> Even if we were not able to weep and lament him on the day on which he was crucified, yet let us now do so at his tomb. But who will roll away the stone for us that is set against the door of the tomb, that we may enter and sit beside him and perform our obligations? . . . But if we cannot, then let us lay beside the door the things which we have brought in remembrance of him, and we will weep and lament until we get home.[1]

We already know what they found. The stone was rolled back. The body was gone. The young man in the dazzling white robe was there. The news was given that the one they had come to bury was very much alive. Mark doesn't say this, but Matthew records that on their way back the women met Jesus, so they saw for themselves that he was indeed among the living.

Isn't that ironic? Women in those days were officially non-persons. They were essentially things, pieces of property. Men had various degrees of status. It could be high. It could be low. Whatever it was, at least they had some. Women had none.

And who was it who first learned of the greatest event in all of human history? Three women who had come to prepare a body for burial, which was a job that no man would ever do. God just doesn't have our sense of values!

Well, that brings us back to where we started. The women were told that Jesus was once again alive, and they were ordered to go tell the disciples ". . . and Peter." Why was Peter singled out?

Among all the disciples, Peter had made the most promises of undying loyalty in the face of danger. Before his arrest Jesus had sadly told the disciples that they were about to be put to the test. They would scatter and run away. Peter was indignant. No, that's not right. Peter wasn't indignant. He was mad! "I'll never leave you. No matter what the others do, I'll stay with you. No one can drive me off. I'll be there, Jesus. You ought to know that."

"Peter, before this night is over, you're going to pretend that you don't even know me."

It happened that way, of course. When Jesus was arrested, Peter ran off with all the rest. Then, during that same night, not once but three times Peter saved his neck by saying, "I don't know what's-his-name." Before he got through, he was even swearing, "Dammit, I don't know that man."

How do you suppose Peter felt when Jesus died? What feelings did Peter have while Jesus was dead in the tomb?

Secret relief, self-justification? "He was just a man after all. It was just as well that I didn't stay with him."

Underneath that I think you'd find guilt. Terrible, terrible guilt. "He was my friend, and I pretended that I didn't even know him."

One person suggested that he might have felt a deep sadness. This person said, "Like the sadness I feel sometimes when I know there are things I could be doing for Christ and I deny him."

Peter surely felt that he deserved to be abandoned by God. After all, he'd abandoned the Son of God.

God saw it differently. "Tell the disciples *and Peter*." Peter!

Peter, who denied having ever known Jesus, received a message from the graveyard that God remembers. Peter is the man God wouldn't forget. "Tell the disciples and Peter."

Isn't that remarkable? The resurrection turns out to be for those who least deserve it.

What do you suppose was Peter's reaction when the news came that Jesus was alive and that Peter had been singled out? What do you think he felt?

Joy? "Wow! That's fantastic! Praise God! He said it, he said it. Now he's done it!"

Amazement? "I can't believe it. I just can't believe it."

Curiosity? "I've got to see that for myself. Get out of my way. I'm going to the cemetery."

Certainly all those things, all mixed together, and a whole lot more.

May he not also have been afraid? May this not in fact have been terrifying news for one who had denied ever having known Jesus? Under those circumstances, do you think you wouldn't be afraid to hear that Jesus was alive and sending the message, "Tell Peter that I'll be seeing him"? I think Peter thought he'd had it.

It's a normal reaction.

If there's any time on earth when the living Jesus is present to encourage us, surely it's when a troubled soul sits down with a concerned pastor to speak privately about sin. Those are times when in a special way the gospel is brought to bear. Confession is made. Pardon is given through the authority of the Scriptures. Forgiveness is received.

Yet it's universally a terrifying experience. Every person that I have dealt with under those circumstances has expressed fear in one way or another—and I am afraid when I speak of my sin to one who pastors me.

I used to wonder about that. Is it something to do with me? Am I really that hard to talk with?

Finally I realized what happens. Though it's not a role that I seek, in that kind of moment the pastor comes to symbolize God and the church. That's likely to be the reason the person is talking with me rather than with some secular counselor. And it is terrifying to be face-to-face with one who symbolizes God and the church and reveal a secret that seems so awful that we feel it surely will make us unacceptable once it's known.

The pain of knowing ourselves and the fear of being known by others is part of the meaning of Jesus alive. A scalpel in the hand of a surgeon is a healing instrument, but first it wounds. Without the wound there is no healing. The resurrection wounds us in order that we may be healed.

There is a sequel to this story. Mark doesn't record it, but we find it in the Gospel of John. Later on the disciples had gone up to Galilee, as they had been told to do. This was essentially a waiting time. Finally the inactivity got to them, and they decided to go fishing. For a time they turned back from being fishers of men and became again fishers of fish.

Just as day was breaking, Jesus appeared on the shore and called instructions that helped them make a large catch. They didn't recognize him at first, but soon they did. Naturally they hurried ashore, where they cooked some fish and had breakfast together. It was a warm, happy reunion, though there was one fact that simply had to dominate everyone's thoughts: Jesus had been dead, and now he was alive. It was so big that they didn't even dare to question him about it.

> When they had finished breakfast, Jesus said to Simon Peter, "Simon, son of John, do you love me more than these?" He said to him, "Yes, Lord; you know that I love you" (John 21:15-19).

A painful question! Peter had made all those promises which he hadn't kept. Now here was Jesus bringing it up. You see, Peter did have reason to be afraid when he heard that Jesus was alive and singling him out. But there was no criticism; simply the instruction, "Feed my lambs."

This was repeated twice more. It was almost like a litany. One has the feeling that each denial needed to be met with its own separate confession and affirmation.

Finally Peter couldn't stand it any more. When Jesus asked a third time, "Do you love me?" Peter broke out, "Lord, you know everything; you know that I love you." Jesus said, "Peter, feed my sheep."

Recently a man said to me that he didn't need to be reminded frequently of his sins. He knew them all too well. He could never seem to get far from the knowledge that the life he lives is much less Christlike than he wants it to be. His need, he said, is to be helped to see how there can be a useful place of Christian service for someone as defective as he knows himself to be.

Peter didn't need to be reminded that he'd failed Jesus. He knew that. How desperately, how bitterly he knew it. He knew that he was a failure. He knew that he'd lost all opportunity to be useful in the kingdom of God. Never could there be a place for anyone like him. Certainly he could never be the leader that Christ had predicted he would be and had trained him to be.

And what was Jesus now saying to him? Over and over, repeating, insisting? "Peter, feed my sheep." Christ intended that Peter be a leader whether he denied him or not.

A deacon in a certain church came to his pastor. The chairman of the deacons, in fact. He was nervous, upset, obviously frightened. He'd come to tell his pastor that he'd become entangled in a situation which would necessarily produce much pain and embarrassment for a number of people within the church. Hearing the first bare facts, it sounded sordid and irresponsible. Certainly it was a situation which should not have been allowed to develop. Yet there it was. It existed, and it had to be dealt with.

Several things became evident. One was that there was no need for the pastor to sit in judgment. The man was judging himself harshly enough. More than anything else he wanted this whole matter brought under Christ. But that seemed hard to do; he thought himself beyond forgiveness.

The effect on the church was another concern. Considering his office, and the fact that the matter involved several parties within the church, it was obvious that it could be very damaging. And so much of his life was wrapped up in the church. He feared that he could no longer be acceptable as a member, let alone a leader.

In truth the church had to wrestle long with its own conscience about that very thing. Where should the church stand? What does the gospel call for?

Finally the church recognized the sincerity of his repentance and voted not only to confirm him as a member, but also to confirm him in his office as chairman of the deacons. The church was saying, "God wouldn't forget you, and we won't either." "Peter, feed my sheep." "Sinner, do God's work."

Those who voted, voted unanimously. Four persons saw how it was going to go, and found this acceptance of one who had fallen to be offensive. They withdrew from the church.

That's Easter. That's resurrection. That's Jesus alive. It *is* offensive to some. It always will be offensive to some. But it's salvation the day you discover that *you* are the person God wouldn't forget.

A Word for Losers (John 8:1-11)

"And Jesus said, 'Neither do I condemn you; go, and do not sin again.'"

Someone once said that failures can be divided into two classes—those who thought and never did and those who did and never thought. As I worked on this sermon, I've had the uneasy feeling that I may have gotten into the latter category, with failure about to follow. Had I thought a little bit more before I announced this sermon, I might more wisely have chosen a different text.

This has to be one of the hardest passages in the Gospels to interpret. You get a clue to that if you just look it up in any modern translation. The *Revised Standard Version* prints the whole thing as a footnote. *The Today's English Version* puts parentheses around it. Others have a footnote which explains that the story of the woman caught in adultery is not in any of the oldest manuscripts. The plain and simple fact is that the story was not written by John, and was not originally a part of John's Gospel.

Of course that doesn't mean that it's not true. The story is very ancient. It can be traced in non-biblical sources to the second century. It sounds like Jesus in every respect. But the fact that it is what scholars like to call a "troubled text" hints at the problems that are going to come when you try to interpret it.

For instance, it's hard to think of a passage in the Gospels that raises more tantalizing questions which simply can't be answered.

The teachers of the law and the Pharisees brought a woman to Jesus. They said, "Teacher, this woman was caught in the very act of committing adultery." Where was her lover? I mean, it takes two to tango. If they caught her in the very act, they must also have caught him. The law called for them both to be killed. Why did they bring only her?

Then we're told that Jesus, asked for an opinion, refused to speak. Instead he just bent over and wrote on the ground with his finger. What did he write? Some say that he only doodled, buying time while he thought. Others suggest that he wrote the ten commandments in the dust, reminding those gathered around that in some way they were all guilty. Others have more lurid imaginations, and they think he wrote specific sins of which each person in the crowd was guilty. But we don't know, we never will know. It's a question that can't be answered.

Sunday evening someone noted that the story says that the crowd left, one by one, "the older ones first." The question was asked, why did they leave in the order of their age? Sunday night I thought maybe it had something to do with manners and customs of the time, but I haven't been able to document that. I don't know why the older ones left first.

It's fair to say that for me this passage has been both maddening and intriguing. It poses all sorts of fascinating questions. I just can't answer many of them.

It's true, though, that as you dig a little deeper into the story of the woman caught in adultery, there are at least some observations which can be made about it.

It's clear that this encounter was intended to be a trap for Jesus. The law of Moses was very specific that people who committed adultery were to be killed. Nowadays you seem a little old-fashioned if you even think that adultery is grounds for divorce, but they took it more seriously in Bible times. Jesus was being tested to see whether or not he would uphold the law and instruct that the woman should be killed. If he did, he would have been violating his own standards of mercy, thereby losing credibility with the crowd. If, instead, he said that she should be set free, he could be charged with disobedience to the law, thereby losing credibility with the crowd.

We can also observe that the sole interest of the teachers of the law and the Pharisees was in "getting" Jesus. They came expressing great concern that the religious principles upon which Israel was founded should be observed. The truth is that, in this instance, they didn't care a bit about the law. If they did, they would also have brought the man. Isn't it interesting how religious people can find religious reasons for doing the most ungodly acts in the name of God?

It should also be clear to us that the woman who was dragged and pulled through the street in public shame and humiliation was a person. A human being. That point, of course, was lost on the religious leaders who brought her there. To them she was simply a means of getting at Jesus. I've noticed that preachers don't always seem to remember that she was a person, either. Some sermons on this text have left me with the uneasy feeling that she didn't really matter, that she was merely a means to the point the preacher wanted to make. Jesus looked at her with wide-open eyes and saw one of God's daughters.

Sunday evening in our group we tried to explore this a bit. We tried to make her come alive in our imaginations as a real person. Of course this is all made up, but we had fun doing it. We named her Rebecca. She did have a name, you know. We'll never know what it really was, but Rebecca's a good name. We decided that she was twenty-two years old and attractively plump. Nobody liked skinny women in those days. We thought that she would have had long, dark hair, dark eyes, and a sexy voice. We agreed that she might have been the third wife of a fat husband who was getting bald. (Just for the record, I thought that remark about him being bald was uncalled for!) We felt sure that she must have been unhappy in her marriage, or she wouldn't have been having an affair. I don't know whether she was anything like that, but she was a person.

As I continued to work with this passage, I found myself off on a side trip. It's intriguing to see how Jesus handled conflict in this instance. You know, when you're in a situation where there's conflict, there are a number of ways you can react. You can get angry. You can use logic to try to show the other person that he's wrong. You can call up your authority and say, "Well, I know I'm right." Sometimes you can throw your opponent off balance with a word or an action which seems irrelevant.

My first church was in a small farming community. Prior to my going there, the church was split. It was one of the nastiest church fights ever, and in a small town naturally everyone gets into the action. In the church there was a kindly old lady named Nanny Bivens. She's dead now, but she was a delightful person—gentle, soft-spoken, mild. In the town there was an old character who had a beard and who chewed tobacco. He wasn't very neat with his tobacco, and the juice was constantly trickling down his chin and staining his beard. It was repulsive.

One day Mrs. Bivens was walking to the store, and she met this fellow. He stopped her, and began to tell her in no uncertain terms what he thought of a church that had such carryin's on. Well, Mrs. Bivens didn't like it either, but she felt it was a family affair, and no business of an outsider—which he was. But that didn't stop him. He kept running down the Baptists at great length and in careful detail. Finally he got all through, and gentle, kindly Nanny Bivens looked him in the eye and, with a razor edge in her voice, asked, "Why don't you wipe your chin?"

The teachers of the law and the Pharisees came to Jesus bringing a woman. They said, "This woman was caught in the very act of committing adultery. In our law, Moses gave a commandment that such a woman must be stoned to death. Now, what do you say?" Jesus didn't say a word. He just bent over and began tracing in the dust with his finger.

Well, that's a side issue. When the unanswerable questions

have been asked, when the obvious has been said, when the side issues have been exhausted, I think there are a pair of truths which are illuminated by this story.

When Eisenhower was President, his chief assistant was Sherman Adams. One afternoon in June, 1958, Sherman Adams delivered a baccalaureate address to a boys' school in New Hampshire. His subject was "The Questions the Bible Tells Us Shall Be Asked on Judgment Day."

> Adams had long been interested in what was going to happen to sinners on that Day. Democrats knew him as the stern moralist who had decried minks, freezers, and influence peddling during Truman's tenure. . . .
>
> Conservative Republicans also resented Adams. They remembered his accusations that Taft was stealing GOP delegate votes in Texas. "Thou shalt not steal," he had cried, wagging a finger at them. To them he was the man who had delivered a ruthless judgment against Air Force Secretary Harold Talbot because he had solicited business for his efficiency engineering firm on official Air Force stationery.[2]

The very afternoon that Adams was delivering that baccalaureate address, testimony was being entered into the record of a House committee that Sherman Adams had accepted bribes. The charges were proved to be true. The "Puritan" had been caught practicing what he had preached against. Suddenly he was left without honor, without integrity, without a base of influence on which to stand.

The teachers of the law and the Pharisees said, "Teacher, this woman was caught committing adultery. The law says she should be killed. What do you say?" Jesus straightened up at last from his scribbling on the ground and said, "Whichever one of you has never done anything wrong may begin the execution." When they heard this they all left, one by one, starting with the eldest. There is illuminated for us the weakness of those who are sure that they are winners. The Pharisees were so confident of their unassailable righteousness that they felt entitled to judge others. With one comment Jesus demolished them. The weakness of those who are confident that they are strong!

That left Jesus and the woman, face-to-face. She literally had no place to hide. She was a loser. I simply can't think of any moment in life that could be more degrading than what she was experiencing. The whole town knew that she was a loser. Jesus knew it. She knew it. No place to hide. A loser.

Jesus said, "Where are they, woman? Is there no one left to

condemn you?" "No one, sir." "Well, then," Jesus said, "I do not condemn you either. You may leave, but do not sin again." There we see illuminated the strength of those who know themselves to be losers, to be without strength. They are the ones who can stand before God making no pretenses, wearing no masks, offering no excuses. They are the ones who find their dignity in the gentleness of the Master. "I don't condemn you either. Just don't sin again."

Perhaps we understand better the position of winners and losers before God if we remember a story Jesus told on another occasion.

> Two men went up to the temple to pray; one was a winner, the other was a loser. The winner stood up and said this prayer to himself: "I thank you, God, that I am not greedy, dishonest, or immoral, like everybody else; I thank you that I am not like that loser. I fast two days every week, and I give you one-tenth of all my income." But the loser stood at a distance and would not even raise his face to heaven, but beat on his breast and said, "O God, have pity on me, a sinner." "I tell you," said Jesus, "this man, and not the other, was in the right with God when he went home" (Luke 18:10-14, adapted).

The teachers of the law and the Pharisees were so sure that they were winners, but they crept away in shame. The woman knew that she was a loser. She went home with Jesus' benediction. If you feel like a loser today, there's a word for you here. Of course there's also a word here for you if you're so sure that everything is right with your life that you can afford to make judgments about others.

Speechless (Mark 9:2-8)

> "And after six days Jesus took with him Peter and James and John, and led them up a high mountain apart by themselves; and he was transfigured before them. . . ."

My name is James. You've all heard of me, though I doubt that you know much about me. You do know that I was privileged to be among the twelve whom Jesus chose to carry on the work he started. I was a disciple. John, who may have been closer to Jesus than anyone else, was my brother.

We had some great times together! We had some bad times, too. There sure are a lot of stories I could tell. Like, for instance, the time we were left speechless. I know that Mark and Matthew and Luke have all written about it, and you've read what they wrote. Even so, maybe you'd like to hear it from me.

The first hint we had that something out of the ordinary was going to happen was when Jesus took Peter and John and me aside and said that next week he'd like to take a day for a retreat. He felt that he needed to get away while he still could and get ready for what he'd have to do later on. He wanted just the three of us to go with him. Naturally we were flattered and honored. I mean, who wouldn't be? We were glad to undertake the traditional six days of purification to get ready for the retreat. It was a little inconvenient, but the discipline was good for us.

I remember that whole period in our lives as a busy time. Puzzling, too. A lot happened that really left us confused.

For instance, there was that moment which the church later came to call "Peter's confession." Jesus had been asking us who people thought he was. Then he asked who we thought he was. The twelve of us had a lot of different ideas, though we were slow to speak up. Suddenly Peter got excited and said, "Why you're the Christ, the one we've been waiting for to save Israel!" Jesus said, "That's right," and congratulated Peter.

That was a strange moment. I'd waited all my life for the Christ to come to save us. Now my friend claimed that he was the one and in some way that I couldn't explain, it made sense. Something inside of me was saying, "That's right! That's right!" Yet in another way it didn't make sense at all. It felt like Truth, and yet it was so big I couldn't get hold of it. Like when you see a puppy trying to grab up a large ball; it's there and it's real, but he can't get his teeth in it. That's the way I felt.

The same thing happened right afterward. Jesus began telling us that he was going to die and be resurrected when we got to Jerusalem. That didn't make any sense at all. I mean the idea of an eventual resurrection wasn't new, except that Jesus seemed to be saying that when you die, you really don't die, but almost immediately have some other kind of life. It was a puzzle.

But to tell you the truth, I don't think we even listened much to that part. We were so confused about his saying that he was going to die. How could he be the Christ and die? He was supposed to save us all. How could he do that if he could be killed?

It was a relief for John and Peter and me to concentrate on the discipline of the six days of purification. That way we couldn't think so much about how bewildered we were. Finally the day came and we started up the mountain.

Church traditions have said that we went up Mt. Tabor. Lots of tourists have visited the top of Mt. Tabor and have been told that it happened there. But it didn't.

In the first place, Mt. Tabor's such a small peak. It's only about one thousand feet high. Jesus seemed to want to get as high as he could, as though he wanted to be especially close to God. Besides, Mt. Tabor had a fort on it in those days, with a garrison and everything. We wanted to be alone.

It was a much higher and lonelier spot to which Jesus led us. I thought we'd never get there. I was so tired before Jesus let us stop that I didn't really care about our retreat anymore.

But eventually we did get there, and we began our retreat. We three disciples sat down close together, although we were lost in our own thoughts. Jesus was off just a little bit by himself. He seemed to want us close, but not too close.

It's hard to explain what happened next. Luke wrote that we were "heavy with sleep" (Luke 9:32), but kept awake. To tell you the truth, I've never been able to describe it exactly, but it was more like we were in a trance, or hypnotized, or something. I don't even know if what we saw happened outside in the "real" world, so to speak, or if it happened within us. It could have been like what happened to Isaiah in the temple when he saw God, but in a vision, so that someone else standing there might not have seen anything. I just don't know, but I know it happened and it was real.

Jesus changed. Right before our eyes he changed. I can't describe it. There aren't any words.

Matthew wrote that Jesus' clothes became "white as light" (Matthew 17:2). Mark said that they were whiter than anyone could ever bleach them (Mark 9:3). I can't improve on that, except to say that what happened to Jesus happened from the inside out. It wasn't just that some spotlight was turned on him, or that heavenly glory was projected onto him. This was from the inside. I felt that we were seeing Jesus just being himself.

The word that best describes what happened to Jesus is the one from which you get your word "metamorphosis." That's what happens when a caterpillar becomes a butterfly. We saw Jesus become indescribably lovely, as a caterpillar becomes a butterfly. He became himself.

Suddenly there was someone else with Jesus. Two someones, really. Moses was there, and Elijah. They died a long time ago, but there they were; obviously not dead, obviously belonging to some order of life which is completely real but which our bodies can't usually perceive.

Think of that! What a meeting that was! Moses was the greatest lawgiver of all time. Elijah was the greatest prophet. They were talking with Jesus. It was as though everything in our entire Jewish history was coming together in Christ.

I remember what they were talking about. They were discussing his "coming departure." It would be through death, but death wouldn't be extinction. Rather death would return him to the vibrant radiance which was his naturally.

Can you understand me if I say that it suddenly made sense of everything, and yet nothing made sense? I mean, I *knew* at that moment that this was the explanation for the death and resurrection he'd talked about. Suddenly it all seemed *right*. Yet, though it fit together deep inside me, later on my mind still hadn't caught up to my heart. It was a long time before my mind understood.

Frankly, we were all struck speechless. John and I couldn't say a word. I don't think we could have made a sound if our lives had depended on it.

Peter was different. Everything affected Peter differently from the rest of us. Peter was speechless, too, except that it was always Peter's way to talk the most when he had the least to say. I've seen some others like that.

Anyway, Peter couldn't stand to be quiet when he didn't know what to say, so he butted right into the conversation which Jesus was having with Moses and Elijah. "Teacher," he said, "it's a good thing that we're here. We'll make three tents, one for you, one for Moses, and one for Elijah." Peter, of course, was thinking of the kind of tent or tabernacle which our ancestors made for God when they were wandering in the wilderness. Peter wanted to provide a place where each of the three could dwell and be worshipped.

I felt instantly that Peter had made a serious mistake, that it would have been better had he just kept quiet. Peter knew it too. When we talked about it later, Peter admitted that he was really seeing Jesus and Moses and Elijah as all being equal. After all, they were all radiant. But they weren't equal.

Suddenly a cloud came up. I don't know where it came from. It was just there. We were in its shadow, and yet, as Matthew mentioned when he wrote about it, it wasn't a dark cloud. It was bright, as though it had its own inner light (Matthew 17:5). This must have been like the pillar of cloud that led Moses and the people through the wilderness. And the voice! I tell you, we heard the voice of God: "This is my beloved Son; listen to him."

Poor Peter would have crawled into the ground had he been able to find a way to do it. It was obvious what that was directed to. Jesus, Moses, and Elijah aren't equal at all. Jesus is even greater, and we should pay attention to him. As if to demonstrate that, Moses and Elijah were suddenly gone. Only Jesus remained. I've often felt since that this is the way it truly is. Great leaders come and go. Only Jesus remains.

We would have stayed there and built our shrines to keep alive the memory of that time on the mountain. Jesus wouldn't let us. Down below there were people who needed us.

It was a long time before I understood what I'd seen. Only after the resurrection did it make sense. Then I realized that after his human death he simply remained what he always had been: the radiant Son of God. I also knew that something similar must be waiting for me. If Moses and Elijah are still living, surely I'm going to keep living too.

So Jesus had given us a great gift. We had a beautiful memory to which we could return when we needed encouragement. We had understanding of things that otherwise would have baffled us forever. We couldn't have found that for ourselves. We could only get it as a gift.

But do you know, I've often wondered: What if we hadn't taken time to go apart with Jesus? We could so easily have missed the moment that left us speechless.

Two Foolish People (I Kings 17:8-16)

"The jar of meal shall not be spent, and the cruse of oil shall not fail, until the day that the LORD sends rain upon the earth."

In the 1930s a traveler who might take a rarely used trail across the Amargosa Desert had only one hope of getting drinking water. At one point on the trail there was a well with an old water pump. If it worked, you could get water. If it didn't you couldn't. It was as simple as that.

This letter was found in a baking powder can wired to the pump handle:

This pump is all right as of June, 1932. I put a new sucker washer into it and it ought to last five years. But the washer dries out and the pump has got to be primed. Under the white rock I buried a bottle of water, out of the sun and cork end up. There's enough water in it to prime the pump, but not if you drink some first. Pour about one fourth and let her soak to wet the leather. Then pour in the rest medium fast and pump like crazy. You'll git water. The well has never run dry. Have faith. When you git watered up, fill the bottle and put it back like you found it for the next feller.

(signed) Desert Pete

P.S. Don't go drinking up the water first. Prime the pump with it and you'll git all you can hold.[3]

What would you do with a letter like that? Suppose that you'd been out on the desert trail under the blistering sun. Suppose that you'd run out of water, and had been only just able to make it to the pump. Your life depends on the decision you make now.

Would you drink the bottle of water and take your chances on the rest of the trail? Would you pour the precious water down a rusty old pump in hopes of getting an unlimited supply back in return?

I suppose it would depend on how much you were willing to trust an unknown character named Desert Pete. It's obvious from the grammar in the letter that he's not too well educated. How much do you suppose he knows about pumps? Would you be willing to bet your life on the strength of his note?

One thing sure: If you were on that trail and found the note, you'd never know whether Desert Pete could be trusted until you'd actually poured that bottle of water down the pump.

Records from the time tell us that some 850 years before the time of Christ there was a widow living with her son. They lived in Phoenicia, which was the next county north of Israel. The widow and son were residents of a village called Zarephath, near the city of Sidon. It was well north on the Mediterranian coast.

It was hard to be a woman without a husband in those days. Unless you had a protector or were willing to turn to prostitution, there wasn't a lot of hope. Often there would simply be no income and no way to get any. In this case the widow and son had utterly exhausted their resources. They'd hoarded every last bite of food to make it last as long as possible, but even so the inevitable had happened. Their food had run out. Since there was a general drought in the area, no one had any to spare. It was a time of famine for the whole land. Certainly no one was going to give anything away to a widow with no protector.

The son was perhaps too young to understand what was happening, but the mother knew well enough. For food they had but a single handful of flour and a small measure of the olive oil that was a staple in their diet. Not enough to feed even one of them, and when it was gone there would be no more. The mother knew. They were about to starve to death.

With a weariness so vast that we who have never been close to starvation can only guess at it, the mother went out to pick up a bit of wood. The time had come to build a fire to cook their final meal. It would take a long time because she couldn't move very fast, but what did time matter anyway? Soon there'd be no more time.

At the edge of the village she saw a man resting. A stranger. She'd never seen him before. Evidently he'd come a long way, for he looked as tired as she felt. He asked a favor of her: "Bring me a drink of water."

That would take more energy, use up strength she didn't have. But on the other hand, she'd been trained all her life that women do what men ask of them. She started to get the drink.

Before she could get very far he called after her, "Bring me a piece of bread too. I haven't eaten."

That was too much. How could she stand that? Her son was dying. She was dying. Now she's supposed to feed some stranger? She couldn't do it. "As the LORD your God lives, I have nothing baked, only a handful of meal in a jar, and a little oil in a cruse; and now, I am gathering a couple of sticks, that I may go in and prepare it for myself and my son, that we may eat it, and die" (1 Kings 17:12).

But the man wouldn't be put off:

> Fear not; go and do as you have said; but first make me a little cake of it and bring it to me, and afterward make for yourself and your son. For thus says the LORD the God of Israel, "The jar of meal shall not be spent, and the cruse of oil shall not fail, until the day that the Lord sends rain upon the earth" (1 Kings 17:13-14).

What would you do if you were the widow? The man was a complete stranger. He sounded confident, as though he knew what he was doing, but you wouldn't have known him. The promise sounds impossible. He would have been trying to get the one thing standing between life and death not only for you, but for your child. Would you have been foolish enough to give him the last of your food? One thing sure, you would never have known whether the man could be trusted until you did as he asked.

There's another side to this story. There was a man in Israel named Elijah. He was a prophet, one who spoke for God. Elijah had the misfortune to live during the reign of King Ahab, who may well have been the worst king Israel ever had. Since Elijah's mission was to be spokesman for God against the king's reckless, faithless foolishness, it was obvious that he wasn't going to be popular at court. Actually King Ahab became Elijah's mortal enemy. From the time that Elijah announced that God was sending a great drought upon the land because Ahab was leading the people in the worship of false gods, Elijah's life wasn't safe. He had to flee to stay alive.

That was a hard time for Elijah. It would seem that one who serves the Lord ought to prosper. That doesn't mean that he ought to be rich, but surely God's servant ought to be able to have enough for him and his family to live on. One who speaks for God should be able to count on God to provide safety and the basic needs of life: a little food and a little shelter. Elijah had to run for his life and hide in the wilderness. It didn't seem fair.

It's true enough that Elijah did survive out in the wilds. The recorded legend is that the birds—the ravens—brought him bits of food morning and night, and he had water to drink from a little brook. Any way you look at it, it wasn't much of a living for a mighty servant of God. And then the brook dried up from the drought. What else could happen?

God finally seemed to notice Elijah's problem. He finally seemed to get around to the needs of his servant. God said, "Elijah, get clear out of this land. Go up to Phoenicia. Near Sidon there's a village called Zarephath. I've ordered a widow there to feed you."

You're ahead of me, aren't you? Elijah was the stranger who met the widow. Elijah was the traveler who asked for water. Elijah was the hungry man who asked for bread, confident that finally he was going to be invited in for a proper meal.

Think of what's been going on in Elijah's mind. From the time the word came to him to leave the wilderness and go to Zarephath surely he's been thinking, "That's more like it. Finally God is taking care of me. Now I'll have proper food to eat. I'll have a place to stay." The world looked suddenly brighter to Elijah.

Now he hears the widow say, "As the LORD your God lives, I have no food." Sitting there, tired to the bone after traveling so far, Elijah must have been numb with shock as he heard those words destroying the hopes with which he'd nourished himself these last weary days. Yet there were words rising within him, words which weren't really his, and yet which wanted to be spoken through his mouth. They were words speaking of things impossible to believe, and yet they insisted on being uttered:

> Fear not; go and do as you have said; but first make me a little cake of it and bring it to me, and afterward make for yourself and your son. For thus says the LORD the God of Israel, "The jar of meal shall not be spent, and the cruse of oil shall not fail, until the day that the Lord sends rain upon the earth."

Could you believe that? Could you say that? If you were standing in Elijah's place, would you be foolish enough to speak such a thing out loud?

What we have here, of course, are two foolish people. Elijah was foolish enough to ask the woman to give him the last bit of food she had. He actually dared tell her that after he ate, there would be enough for her and her son. For her part, she was foolish enough to believe him. She actually gave Elijah the last bit of food she had in the world. Two foolish people.

> . . . she went and did as Elijah said; and she, and he, and her household ate for many days. The jar of meal was not spent, neither did the cruse of oil fail, according to the word of the LORD which he spoke by Elijah (1 Kings 17:15-16).

Isn't that something? God had provided for both of them, but neither would have ever known it if Elijah hadn't asked and the woman given at a time when both the asking and the giving seemed utterly foolish.

Nearly two thousand years ago a baby was born in an obscure village. The circumstances of that birth were rather embarrassing. The neighbors knew how to count in those days as well as they do today. A decent number of months had not passed between the marriage of Joseph and Mary and the birth of their first child.

In due time the child grew into a man, and the man was a misfit. He just didn't quite belong. He left a good respectable carpenter shop in order to wander the countryside as an itinerant teacher. And the things he taught! He claimed to be the Son of God. He said that if people would just forget everything else and do as he taught they'd have peace beyond all understanding and something he called "abundant life."

It got so embarrassing that his family were certain that he'd gone crazy, and they tried to put him away. Eventually he made such a nuisance of himself that the authorities decided to get rid of him. They judged him a criminal and had him executed.

But that didn't end it. Some who'd been with him claimed that he only stayed dead for a little while. They said he came to life again, and that people who believed that he was still alive and who lived by his teachings instead of by ordinary common sense would also come alive in a way they'd never known before. In fact, it's still being said.

But is it true?

There's only one way you'll ever know.

Notes

Notes to Chapter 1

[1] William Manchester, *The Death of a President* (New York: Harper and Row, 1967), p. 189.

[2] Marshall McLuhan, *Understanding Media: The Extensions of Man* (New York: McGraw-Hill Book Co., 1964), p. 33.

[3] The author is indebted to Merrill R. Abbey, *Communication in Pulpit and Parish* (Philadelphia: Westminster Press, 1973), pp. 71-72.

[4] Herman Melville, *Moby Dick* (New York: The Modern Library, 1930), pp. 55-56.

[5] Clyde Reid, *The Empty Pulpit* (New York: Harper and Row, Publishers, 1967), p. 77.

[6] Fred B. Craddock, *As One Without Authority* (Enid, Oklahoma: Phillips University Press, 1971), p. 54. Used by permission of Abingdon Press.

[7] *Ibid.*, p. 28. This comment is based on work reported by Charles E. Benda, "Language, Consciousness and Problems of Existential Analysis," *American Journal of Psychotherapy*, vol. 14, no. 2 (April, 1960).

[8] Reuel L. Howe, *The Miracle of Dialogue* (Greenwich, Connecticut: The Seabury Press, 1963), p. 20.

[9] Browne Barr, *The Well Church Book* (New York: The Seabury Press, 1976), p. 56.

[10] *Ibid.*, p. 58.

[11] *Ibid.*, p. 63.

[12] Halford E. Luccock, *Communicating the Gospel* (New York: Harper & Brothers, 1954), p. 139.

[13] Frank E. X. Dance and Carl E. Larson, *Speech Communication* (New York: Holt, Rinehart and Winston, 1972), p. 168.

[14] A full discussion of "assimilation-contrast effects" may be found in Carolyn Sherif, Muzafar Sherif and Roger Nebergall, *Attitude and Attitude Change: The Social Judgement-Involvement Approach* (Philadelphia: W. B. Saunders Co., 1965), p. 15.

[15] Clement Welsh, *Preaching in a New Key* (Philadelphia: Pilgrim Press, 1974), p. 111.

[16] Clyde E. Fant, Jr., and William M. Pinson, Jr., *20 Centuries of Great Preaching, Volume 6: Spurgeon to Meyer, 1834-1929* (Waco, Texas: Word Books, 1971). p. 32.

[17] *Ibid., Volume 12: Marshall to King, 1902-*, p. 318.

[18] Reuel L. Howe, *Partners in Preaching: Clergy and Laity in Dialogue* (New York: Seabury Press, 1967), pp. 34-35. Copyright © 1967 by The Seabury Press Inc.

[19] *Ibid.*, p. 35.

[20] *Ibid.*, p. 36.

[21] *Ibid.*, p. 45.

[22] Howe, *Miracle of Dialogue*, pp. 56-66.

Notes to Chapter 2

[1] David M. Granskou, *Preaching on the Parables* (Philadelphia: Fortress Press, 1972), p. 3.

[2] Joachim Jeremias, *The Parables of Jesus* (New York: Charles Scribner's Sons, 1962), p. 21.

[3] James D. Smart, *The Old Testament in Dialogue with Modern Man* (Philadelphia: Westminister Press, 1964), pp. 11-12. Copyright © MCM LXIV by W. L. Jenkins. Used by permission of Westminster Press.

[4] *Ibid.,* p. 24.

[5] Fred B. Craddock, *As One Without Authority* (Enid, Oklahoma: Phillips University Press, 1971) p. 71.

[6] Courtney Anderson, *To The Golden Shore* (Boston: Little, Brown & Company, 1956), pp. 56-57. Copyright © 1956 by Little, Brown & Company. Assigned to Author, 1963. Used by permission of Zondervan Publishing House.

[7] Keith Miller, *A Second Touch* (Waco, Texas: Word Books, 1967), p. 18.

[8] John Killinger, *The Centrality of Preaching in the Total Task of Ministry* (Waco, Texas: Word Books, 1969), p. 24.

[9] Karl Barth, *The Preaching of the Gospel,* trans. B. E. Hooke (Philadelphia: Westminster Press, 1963), p. 16.

[10] Killinger, op. cit., p. 23.

[11] Dietrich Ritschl, *A Theology of Proclamation* (Richmond: John Knox Press, 1963), pp. 20-21.

Notes to Chapter 3

[1] Reuel L. Howe, *Partners in Preaching: Clergy and Laity in Dialogue* (New York: Seabury Press, 1967), pp. 68-70. Copyright © 1967 by The Seabury Press Inc.

[2] Robert R. Rathbone, *Communicating Technical Information* (Reading, Mass.: Addison-Wesley Co., 1966), pp. 44-45.

[3] Robert W. Duke, "The Sermon as One of the Mass Media," *The Christian Ministry,* Vol. IV, No. 4 (July, 1973), p. 10.

[4] Helmut Theilicke, *The Trouble with the Church,* trans. John W. Doberstein (New York: Harper & Row, Publishers, 1965), p. 25.

[5] Carl R. Rogers, *On Becoming a Person: A Therapist's View of Psychotherapy* (Boston: Houghton Mifflin Co., 1961), p. 33.

[6] Interview with Dr. Fred B. Craddock, Professor of New Testament and Preaching at the Graduate Seminary of Phillips University, Enid, Okla. The interview took place at Eugene, Ore., January 13, 1976.

[7] Joseph Heinemann, ed., *Literature of the Synagogue* (New York: Behrman House, 1975), p. 108.

[8] William Barclay, *Communicating the Gospel* (Sterling, Scotland: The Drummond Press, 1968), pp. 34-35.

[9] *Ibid.,* pp. 30-31.

[10] Clement Welsh, *Preaching in a New Key* (Philadelphia: United Church Press, 1974), p. 30.

[11] *Ibid.,* pp. 32-33.

[12] Henry H. Mitchell, *Black Preaching* (Philadelphia: J.B. Lippincott Co., 1970), p. 98.

[13] *Ibid.,* pp. 197-198.

[14] Duane Mehl, "Mass Media and the Future of Preaching," *Concordia Theological Monthly,* 1970, Vol. XLI, No. 4, p. 210.

[15] Howe, *Partners in Preaching,* pp. 71-72.

Notes to Chapter 4

[1] Fred B. Craddock, *As One Without Authority* (Enid, Oklahoma: Phillips University Press, 1971), p. 82.

[2] Carl R. Rogers, *On Becoming a Person: A Therapist's View of Psychotherapy* (Boston: Houghton Mifflin Co., 1961), p. 53.

[3] Dean C. Barnlund, ed., *Interpersonal Communication: Survey and Studies* (Boston: Houghton Mifflin Co., 1968), pp. 252-257.

[4] Clyde Reid, *The Empty Pulpit* (New York: Harper and Row, Publishers, 1967), p. 87-89.

[5] James D. Smart, *The Old Testament in Dialogue with Modern Man* (Philadelphia: Westminster Press, 1964), p. 8.

[6] Halford E. Luccock, *Communicating the Gospel* (New York: Harper & Brothers, 1954), p. 126.

[7] Clyde E. Fant, Jr., and William M. Pinson, Jr., *20 Centuries of Great Preaching, Volume 8: Morgan to Coffin, 1863–1959* (Waco, Texas: Word Books, 1971), VIII, p. 226.

[8] A. J. Gossip, "But When Life Tumbles In, What Then?" in *ibid.*, p. 235. Used with permission of T. & T. Clark, Limited.

[9] *Ibid.*, p. 237.

[10] *Ibid.*, pp. 238-239.

[11] For a fuller discussion of problem solution organization see J. Daniel Baumann, *An Introduction to Contemporary Preaching* (Grand Rapids: Baker Book House, 1972), pp. 79-80.

Notes to Chapter 5

[1] Burton H. Throckmorton, ed., "Gospel of Peter," 12:50 ff., *Gospel Parallels: A Synopsis of the First Three Gospels* (New York: Thomas Nelson, 1957), p. 187.

[2] William Manchester, *The Glory and the Dream* (Boston: Little, Brown and Company, 1973), pp. 1022-1023.

[3] Keith Miller and Bruce Larson, *The Edge of Adventure* (Waco, Texas: Word Books, 1974), p. 29.